The Formula
How to be your very best self

Maria Burke

Copyright © 2021 by Maria Burke

978-1-9993660-3-2

All rights reserved. This book or any portion thereof may not be reproduced or used in any manner whatsoever without the express written permission of the publisher except for the use of brief quotations in a book review.

Names and identifying details have been changed to protect the privacy of individuals.

Published in Ireland by Maria Burke Publishing.

About the Author

Maria Burke is a high-performance coach, entrepreneur, pharmacy graduate and author, Maria holds a BSc in pharmacy from Trinity College in Dublin, Ireland, an Advanced Diploma in Executive Coaching and a Certificate in Cognitive Behavioural Therapy.

An experienced businesswoman, Burke owned and managed three retail pharmacies as well as her own wholesale and distribution business, working with such leading global brands as OPI, St. Tropez, Neal's Yard Remedies and Smashbox Cosmetics.

In the latter part of 2020, Burke established Waywords Journals; books, journals and planners beautifully designed in Ireland, whose purpose is to help people find their way with words by using journaling for their own desired purpose.

In her free time, Burke enjoys being outdoors, which she feels enhances her clarity, energy, and focus. Burke lives in Dublin, Ireland, with her husband and daughter.

You can connect with her at www.waywordsjournals.com.

To my husband, Niall McHugh, for encouraging me to write this book, and to my wonderful daughter, Holly, for whom I am grateful every single day.

To my family, all of you, for just being there.

Contents

About the Author iii

Introduction: The Story.. ix

Chapter 1: The Results Rift: What's Possible with Connection, Clarity, Confidence, and Conviction 1

Connection, Clarity, Confidence, and Conviction—The Way to Results You Want 5

What Is Confidence Anyway, and Why Do We Need It?...................7

The Dreaded Lack of Confidence… 8

Say Yes to Carrots 13

The Amazing Apollo 13 Team... 15

When You Try, It's Great to Succeed.. 17

Chapter 2: The Pathway to Success 21

The Results Catalyst—Five Practical Steps to Success...................... 24

Freedom from Negative Beliefs 25

Work in Accordance with Your Values 26

Mistakes Are a Great Way to Learn 27

Formulate Your Own Purpose Statement.................................... 30

Chapter 3: Know and Appreciate the Real You.................................31

Make Room for Joy 33
Celebrate Your Uniqueness 35
Are You Living Your Best Life? 37

Chapter 4: Find the Evidence—The Positives for Positivity 39

Positive Attitudes—Higher Sales 40
We Have More Potential Than We Realise 41
Positivity—To Help with Challenges 42
Your Personal Evidence for Positivity Worksheet 43

Chapter 5: What on Earth's Stopping You?...................................45

Starting Small Can Result in Big Changes 47
Gathering Your Own Evidence.. 48

Chapter 6: Results Catalyst—The Formula for Freedom Beckons 51

Freedom from Limiting Beliefs 52
Realise the Effectiveness of Playing to Your Strengths 55
Work to Your Values... 56
The Magic Ingredient: Create Your Own Purpose Statement.. 59
Now You Have the Tools to Set New, Realisable Goals.................... 61

Chapter 7: The Business of Happiness 64

So, Happiness—What's It All About? 65

Ah, the Joy of Happiness… 66
What's Your Happiness Formula? 70
Dig Deep to Find Your Joy 71

Chapter 8: The DO IT Programme for Action and Results 73

Make Decisions That Matter 74
Organise to Get the Results You Need 76
Implement Your Plans 77
Treat Yourself 78

Chapter 9: Habits, Habits, Habits, Habits, Habits 80

Healthy Habits 80
    Exercise 81
    Eating Well 84
    Sleep 84
Speed Up Good Habit Formation 86
Practical Tools to Embed Habits 86
    The Daily Five Thank Yous 87
    Choose Habits That Matter 89
    Build Routines 89
Daily, Weekly, Monthly Action Plan for
Embedding Better Habits 92
    Your Daily Action Plan 92
    Your Weekly Action Plan 92
    Your Monthly Action Plan 92

Chapter 10: Result: Connected to Your Success 94

Get Out Your Spade and Dig Deep 95
Where's Your Joy? 97
Be Delighted with Who You Are.. 98
Live Life with Greater Ease 99

Acknowledgements 101

Please Review 102

INTRODUCTION

The Story

I've owned various retail and wholesale distribution businesses through the years. With each one, there were times when I wondered what the hell I was doing. There were successes, failures, adventures, fun, challenges, new experiences, meeting lots of different people, travel, and now and then, boredom. I visited the Middle East, Africa, Europe, and the United States for business meetings and conferences. I loved it sometimes, hated it others, and on some level, I wanted to do something else; I just didn't know what.

The successes were great, yet I learned more from my mistakes, so much so that I eventually started to appreciate the failures! Weird, right? Especially, as I live in Ireland, where, as a culture, we frown upon failure—although we're getting better. Still, my feelings about the opportunities failure has presented don't strike me as strange, really, because in addition to learning, these failures have built character—and resilience. And I've always admired character, which to me means being someone with depth and stories to tell—stories with challenge and danger, with interesting people and a happy ending, or at least an exciting ending. As a child, you may have had the experience of your parents meeting friends on the street or their friends coming to visit your home, and the adults would tell colourful tales from long ago about adventures they'd had, things that had gone wrong, and stories that were just plain funny. If you're like me, these times made a strong impression.

Everyone loves a good story. Recently, I was putting my energetic six-year-old nephew to bed, after his sister and my daughter had given up. The only thing that calmed him down were stories of his dad, my brother, when he was a child. My own daughter now thinks that my childhood stories of growing up on a farm—being chased by a bull, being driven around on tractors and trailers, milking cows, and jumping on hay bales—are way more interesting than her own stories of life on the edge of Dublin city centre.

My mum and dad are great storytellers. As a child and teenager, I marvelled at how they even remembered enough of what had happened twenty and thirty years earlier to be able to tell these amazing stories. During those years, I couldn't imagine ever having so many stories to share, and I yearned to one day have my own, ones that built the character I so badly sought. I always wanted to have lived through enough to come out the other side, to be that someone with an interesting story to tell. Back then, I thought only of the adventures I'd experience to be able to create these fascinating stories. I never thought of the pain that may be involved.

During my varied business careers, I forgot about this desire to live a life full of stories to tell. For some time, I viewed my mistakes as failures, rather than as experiences to learn from. One midwinter day, I stood in my warehouse, which housed a forklift I was very proud of, and various other gadgetry to move and stack pallets of make-up, skincare products, and all sorts of lotions and potions. I was having a discussion—more accurately an argument—with one of my warehouse employees, probably about the untidy warehouse or an urgent order that hadn't been dispatched on time (again) because he had focused on less important but easier jobs instead.

We were so different that our paths never would have crossed if I hadn't set up my wholesale distribution business. While our beliefs and take on life couldn't have differed more, he was an interesting, colourful character, a storyteller (!), and he told really funny jokes. The guy never, ever, ate vegetables—ever—and seemed to think that anytime I asked him to keep a more organised warehouse, my sole purpose was to create more work for him. Suddenly, as I looked at him that day, I thought, *OMG. What on earth am I doing here, having this pointless conversation, with this person who's not even listening?* Immediately, though, I remembered my desire to experience enough of life to have interesting stories to share. I totally lost my train of thought and started to laugh as I realised—ha! *Boy, do I have stories to tell now*. It hit me there and then that because I had these various experiences, the highs and the lows that had led me from my retail businesses to my wholesale distribution business, I finally had stories to tell. The mistakes were not failures; they were, as I've said, character-building.

Of course, there were more ups and downs after that realisation; navigating businesses through the latest recession, which was tougher and certainly lasted longer than I expected, was not easy, yet adopting the view that this was all a new learning opportunity helped me get through. And the good news: I learned how to cut costs to the bone—fast—focus for longer hours, improve stock control, decrease debtor days, implement sales processes, motivate teams despite low morale due to the economy, and so much more. Excel spreadsheets became my friend. I was always aware of the importance of looking after our customers, but during this period it became even more crucial. In fact, I wondered why I hadn't run things so efficiently before the recession hit—Aha! I guess I'm not the only one who wondered this at that time.

I wanted to share these experiences with you from a place of knowing that even though life has its ups and downs, the downs are okay. This book is a combination of stories from which I've learned valuable lessons and coaching tools I find genuinely helpful for connecting with what's important in life and in business. These are some of the tools I use myself and with my clients daily to develop clarity and confidence. They've enabled my clients and me to live life with more ease and a sense of purpose. Of course, it's not always easy to take risks and weather failure, yet these two steps are absolutely necessary to pursue your dreams and build rich stories of your own. The issues tackled in this book are universal: from New York to New Delhi, from Paris to Philadelphia, people experience doubts and fears. I hope that when you read this book, you'll develop a stronger sense of who you are; understand what's important to you; set more meaningful, achievable goals; and get, with greater ease, the results you want in life. In short, I hope this book will help you be your very best self.

CHAPTER 1

The Results Rift: What's Possible with Connection, Clarity, Confidence, and Conviction

All our dreams come true if we have the courage to pursue them.
—Walt Disney

Are you clear about what you want from life and what's best for you—in the way of family, career, health, and happiness? What does success in these areas mean to you? I love that question, because focusing on the answer is essential to guiding your choices in life, helping you to navigate business situations, and indeed for creating and reaching all our goals.

When we don't know what we want and how to go about getting it, there's often a gap between our expectations and what actually happens. I call this the "results rift." Without this rift, *every* company would succeed, every product launch would go according to plan, and we would all live in the homes of our dreams in a safe and peaceful world. So how do we bridge the gap between the goals set and what actually happens? Is there a straightforward method?

Studies show that gaps between actual results and expectations often occur because of unclear objectives, poor communication, lack of commitment, unrealistic goals being set in the first place, and lack of personal ownership and buy-in. Of course there's a solution to each of these issues, and I believe to live and work at our best, each one of us must start by being clear about our own objectives, knowing what matters to us, and how best to use our strengths. We must know our own purpose in life. We can then take this knowledge about ourselves and use it to live our best lives and to choose the right career path, giving our very best to both and getting the results we want for ourselves and the business results to which we have committed.

One of my happiest moments was when I reached the summit of Mt. Kilimanjaro, after spending five days hiking, scrambling, climbing, squashed in a tent, with no shower, no toilet facilities, among mice and rats, often feeling sick, and sometimes dizzy. I had a pain in my chest, was absolutely filthy, and I smelled (I didn't realise how much until everyone got into the enclosed space of the bus on the way back to our hotel when we had completed the climb). And I was exhausted like never before. Yet I was absolutely 100 percent happy. There was no doubt—this felt great.

How could that be? Well, I'd achieved a very clear goal within a defined timeline. My confidence was high—I'd reached the top of Africa, despite every hardship along the way. And there were hardships. Physically exhausted, the altitude and oxygen levels made even the smallest tasks—like lifting my arm to take a photo—impossibly hard. The physical exhaustion was one thing, but staying mentally strong enough through the long days, especially as we climbed higher and oxygen levels depleted, we all agreed, was the big deal. If we were to make it, we couldn't allow our minds to shut down before our bodies did for even a second.

There were eleven of us. Before we left on the trip, we agreed that if any one of us succumbed to severe altitude sickness, we wouldn't endanger our health. We'd follow well-known medical advice, and that person would descend to lower altitude with higher oxygen levels. However, we also made a deal that we would all work together to make it to the top and that we would do all we could to help one another get there. With that resolution, we set off with great hope, positivity, and a sense of adventure.

Yet when we arrived and looked up at the top of the tallest mountain in Africa, the summit lost in the clouds, I realised that the size of this task was far bigger than I'd perceived or trained for. Looking for outside reassurance, which, in hindsight, really meant nothing (yet I wanted it), I asked our guide, "What are the odds for all of us making it to the top?" He looked around at our group, then looked me up and down, and said, "I'm not sure." It wasn't a confident "I'm not sure."

It was the way he looked at me that made me wonder if I'd bitten off more than I could chew. But then I decided, *Hmmph. He doesn't know me or my friends.* Why had I even asked him anyway? I realised that no matter what anyone else thought or said, only my own mind and my own legs could do the job. We could make it. As with any team, we needed to pull together, to support one another—this was crucial to our success. And, as with all teams, everyone had to do their own work to the best of their ability. I decided once again, even after seeing the actual magnitude of the task, that I was going to reach the top. I believed it was possible. And it was. The teamwork worked. Everyone did their best, and we all made it. Result, according to expectations. No gap, no results rift.

That moment, at the top of Africa, shared with my new husband and some long-time, wonderful friends, was one I still hold as one of my absolute favourites. The conviction I'd had that I could do the climb paid off. And it was worth it. Anything is possible with clarity, confidence, conviction—and a plan. And the connection to yourself, where you *feel* that this, whatever "this" is, is exactly the right thing to do in your life, at that moment.

I remember so clearly the moment the opportunity presented itself for me to climb Mt. Kilimanjaro. It was a sunny Saturday afternoon in Dublin. A friend called, saying he and some others were going to climb in September, and planned to summit with the full moon. He didn't even have to ask whether I was interested; I was there already! I was so excited, I immediately said yes. I didn't have to think about it for a second. Then I convinced my husband-to-be that climbing Mt. Kilimanjaro would be amazing—let the adventure begin.

You know those moments that come along where you're absolutely sure that this idea and choice is right, the timing is perfect, and there are no doubts? Imagine if you could have more of those moments. If you could be so connected to an idea, really clear it's the right one for you or your business, and have the confidence to take the actions you need to get there? That was the case when I climbed Kilimanjaro with my friends and with any of the businesses I ever ran. Whether it was retail, wholesale distribution, training, or Internet sales, when I always found that having worked to clear goals and targets with confident, deliverable plans, where the team was absolutely equipped with the tools to succeed, the results rift was a lot less than when we didn't. Often, when we perfected our formula and added in some good luck, there was no results rift at all. That always felt great!

Connection, Clarity, Confidence, and Conviction— The Way to Results You Want

Being **clear** about what you want in life is essential. Exploring your inner **connection** to your plans, checking in to feel if it's absolutely right, is critical. Once you have the clarity and connection, you need the **confidence** to achieve your goal. And that comes with practice. If you want to be great at something, to do anything, it's possible to learn how. You want to be a great leader? You really want it? Great. Once you're clear on this goal, 100 percent connected to the idea, no doubts, then learn how. I have so many examples of how knowledge and learning builds confidence (some of which come later in this book). Tony Schwartz, author of *Be Excellent at Anything: The Four Keys to Transforming the Way We Work and Live*, mentions that insecurity plagues consciously or subconsciously every human being he's ever met and that the best way to build confidence in a given area is to invest energy in it and work hard at it—to practice it. Confidence is, after all, essential to achieving goals in all areas of life.

Throughout my life, I've had areas where I lacked confidence. In business, especially at the start, I really believed I didn't have what it took to succeed. I worried all the time that I'd be a complete failure. I lost sleep, didn't eat at times, and overate at other times. Lack of confidence is an absolute pain in the ass, at best—a waste of valuable thinking time, a major waste of energy. A lack of confidence absolutely indicates that you're not making the most of your life. How could you be, when your productive time and energy are taken up with lack-of-confidence thoughts?!

My lack of confidence in business, while holding me back in some ways, also sparked a huge interest in learning how to overcome it, which led to success. With Kilimanjaro, I was deeply connected to the idea, I read up on what physical training was necessary (did enough training to believe this was possible), and our team had a clear plan—all of which gave me the confidence to reach that goal and experience one of the most amazing moments of my life.

With the formula below, your life will change for the better. It's possible to get the results you want in whatever area of life you want them. No matter what the results you're aiming for. This principle works across the board.

The ingredients to find this confidence, to close the gap, the rift between expectations and results are as follows:

1. Connect to yourself.
2. Get clarity about what you want.
3. Set clear, measurable goals with a defined timeline.
4. Create a plan for success.
5. Find the confidence to believe you can and will do it.

Each one of you is reading this book for a different reason. Maybe something's holding you back in your career. Maybe you're getting in your own way socially. Or you just can't say no, which is leading to you feeling overwhelmed. Life is complicated. If you know what you want and you're not getting there, you're going to need to find a way to believe you can reach your goals, find the confidence that helps you take action, and be true to yourself. For example, if your goal is to buy that new house that just aligns with who you are, and know you can afford it, you want to find the confidence to know that you will indeed be successful enough in your career to make the mortgage repayments. Same thing applies if you want to wear that fabulous bright-red dress you know makes you look great—yet will get you more attention than you like. Find the confidence to do it. Connection and confidence are essential for all of us to live lives that are true to ourselves—whatever that life may be. But we're all unique; success and confidence mean different things to everyone. It takes confidence to remain true to yourself, to give that killer presentation or start your own business. It takes confidence to be your very best self.

Each of you is coming at this challenge from a different angle, with different values and goals, and with diverse hopes and dreams. Different factors are contributing to your perceived lack of confidence in whatever area affects you the most. Maybe it's a belief that you're not capable, or you feel too vulnerable to negative outside influences, or you lack experience, or you feel you're unable to achieve what you set out to do—everyone's reasons will be their own. But whatever the reason, you need confidence to reach your goal.

What Is Confidence Anyway, and Why Do We Need It?

For me, confidence is a feeling…a feeling of being comfortable, and at one with the world. I also like author, coach, and motivational speaker Susan Murphy's quote: "Confidence is a belief in your ability to succeed—a belief that stimulates action."

Makes sense, right? If you don't believe you can do something, why try it in the first place? But if you truly believe you can do something, then you will. In the game of golf, they say that the farthest distance on a golf course is the distance between your two ears. I don't play golf but can relate to this saying when I decide to put a target time on a 10k run, which I do every now and then just to see if I still can reach that particular time.

You're all either working for a corporation, running your own business, raising a family, or running a household—doing *something*, trying to succeed. Because you're trying, you must, somewhere inside, believe you'll succeed. Even if it's only a kernel of belief, it's there. If you carry around the belief that you may not succeed, you feel stressed, right? Your expected results won't come as easily without the belief that you'll succeed. The route won't be as straightforward.

For many, this belief in their ability to succeed is challenged daily—hourly even—by many of the 70,000 thoughts some researchers say we have each and every day. Factoring in seven hours sleep, that's 4,000 conscious and unconscious thoughts running through your brain every waking hour. Having confidence is undermined by negative self-talk. Imagine if even half of the 4,000 thoughts are negative! In her book *Flourishing*, Maureen Gaffney states that it takes five positive actions to balance just one negative one. It makes sense that this same formula holds true for our thoughts. So it's important for your self-talk to be positive. Enough other people will be the naysayers—there's no need for you to be!

The Dreaded Lack of Confidence…

Everyone is different, yet the issue of confidence affects most people in some area of life and work. Confidence wasn't something I thought about until I started my own business. I didn't think about clarity, either. My college course didn't involve imagination—qualifying as a pharmacist is just about facts. My dial was pretty much set to happiness. Any sad times were temporary. However, when I graduated and started working, I suddenly developed a real sense of responsibility. I found it hard to adjust to the weight of my responsibilities and started to worry.

It didn't help this newfound sense of responsibility when I started my own business at twenty-three years old, a retail pharmacy in an Irish country village where I knew nobody. I didn't really know why I started it; it just seemed a good idea at the time. But I now had a bank loan and the responsibility of running a business. And I didn't have a clue how to run it, but I'd gone ahead, figuring I could sell my pharmacy in three to five years and travel if I decided I didn't like it. I had a "ready, fire, aim" sort of attitude back then—thoughts like "what if this fails" came later on.

No new business starts out an immediate success, but I didn't know that then. So, when making bank-loan repayments became an issue each month, the worries just took over. I spent hours alone in a quiet country pharmacy. I felt isolated and lost confidence socially (being alone for hours in a quiet country pharmacy didn't help) and started to wonder about confidence as a life skill. I also started to have unhappy feelings from time to time.

I was just twenty-four years old and suddenly not living the life I had expected or wanted. Because of my circumstances, I became highly focused on finding out what makes people confident and happy. I read books, went to seminars, and asked people, many of whom thought I was going a bit daft. It wasn't the type of conversation that friends, customers (I didn't have colleagues), and family were used to. Some of the books I read—the old favourites like *Feel the Fear and Do It Anyway* and *The Road Less Travelled*—were really great, and they offered a window into a world I had not previously explored.

Because my first business took some time to build, I began to wonder whether I was good enough to be in business. I worried that I was doing everything wrong. Even though my confidence and happiness levels had decreased, no one probably realised I was less happy and confident. Outwardly, I was still the same. That disparity started me thinking about how other people coped with adult life's responsibilities, what factors determined confidence, happiness, and success.

With the first pharmacy not going so well, with no possibility of repaying my bank loans, I felt trapped. If I closed down the store, I'd still have the debt—I knew I needed more customers. So, when an opportunity came to open a second pharmacy in a bigger town, a much busier location, I decided to go ahead. I convinced my bank manager not from a place of confidence, more from a feeling I had no other choice, that the larger store with more traffic would help cash flow and profits, move slow stocks, and enable me to increase profit margins by buying in volume. It worked. I got another loan. Just enough to get going. By then, I knew owning pharmacies wasn't exactly what I wanted to do with my life, but I felt if I could succeed with the second shop and sell out in a few years, then I could do what I wanted to, which at the time, in my mid-twenties, was to travel the world and think about a career later. I was going to "slug it out" for a while longer.

Here began a few years of hard work, long hours, bigger bank loans, high interest rates, and pressure. I started an MBA programme but didn't finish it because my entire life was taken up with work and study. I cried a lot (even, to my eternal embarrassment, in front of the bank manager) and still felt trapped, but I didn't really honestly ask myself what I could or would do about it.

At this stage in my life, I really didn't want to be saddled with so many responsibilities. I didn't feel confident, yet I managed somehow to find enough clarity to succeed at my business. I'd seen how with a second pharmacy business was better, and the economies of scale were working. For a while, I pushed aside how I felt and worked on a financial plan with the medium-term goal of moving on.

The second pharmacy was going quite well, so I decided to buy a third pharmacy. I closed the original shop because it was a drain on resources, and still not doing well. Things were busy, lots of pressure, and then suddenly there was a lot of chatter in the sector about the increased value of retail pharmacies. So I decided to focus on sales, profit margins, and stock control in my shops, and then sell. I told myself I'd give it a year. It only took me six months to build the business to where it needed to be to get the price I wanted. I had a very clear goal and knew what I needed to do to reach that goal. I successfully sold one pharmacy quickly, at the height of the market for a higher price than I'd expected. At thirty-one years old, I held in my hand a cheque for €1.4 million (approximately $1.7 million). This was the year 2000. I remember the moment as though it happened yesterday, the huge feeling of relief, of instantly a weight being lifted from my shoulders, a sense of possibility. Of course, I also felt confidence and an amazing feeling of a job well done.

Less than a year later, I sold the second pharmacy, for almost the same price. These were exciting times. Once again, I was connected to what I wanted—it felt right. I had set a clear goal (increasing profits and selling the business) and a defined timeline for reaching that goal. The numbers showed I could meet the goal and the timeline; that confirmation helped me create a plan, which gave me the confidence to succeed at that particular task.

It took me a few more years to embed the lessons I learned on clarity, connection, confidence, and conviction in more areas of my life and work. I didn't take enough time to decide what was next, and without thinking twice, I jumped into another business, this time supplying into retail. The idea came to me. It was a good one but I didn't **connect** to what I really wanted to do with my life at that time. This later caused so much stress and often rather sizeable "results rifts." I often had the **conviction** but **clarity** and **confidence** took longer to work their way into my daily habits. There are many ups and downs in life and in business—for everyone. Lack of clarity resulted in the failure of various businesses I was involved in, including a retail aromatherapy outlet and a make-up and skincare training academy. Lack of confidence caused human resource (HR) and communication issues for me, too—I valued advice from the wrong people, trusted certain employees who took advantage of that trust.

Conviction and courage were never a problem for me. I really and truly believe that if you want something badly enough, then you can absolutely make it happen. But it's necessary to be 100 percent clear that what you think you want is actually want you really want. You need to connect with it. Also, without the confidence that you have what it takes to achieve your goals—whether they're in leadership, entrepreneurial pursuits, public speaking (this is a biggie for many people), sports, social areas, or whatever you desire—there's no way on earth it's going to happen. To make it happen, you need a plan, and you need to act on that plan. Certainly, nobody else will do it for you. It's 100 percent up to you, and the reward is worth every effort.

Each and every day in business, and in other areas of one's life, people experience a gap between expected results and the actual reality. As I've mentioned, I have owned and managed a number of businesses—some succeeded, others failed, with the failures always due to a gap between sales and other expectations versus what actually happened. Every other day in the news there are stories about companies not delivering on profits according to expectations. Around 80 percent of new businesses fail within eighteen months. In my experience, a lack of clarity and communication are often the cause.

Success comes when a business operates with connection and clarity, confidence, and the conviction that what you're setting out to achieve is possible.

Say Yes to Carrots

Another of my favourite success examples is about when I was running my wholesale sales and marketing business. With every brand we worked with I always wanted to do the very best we could. This story has all four elements—connection, clarity, confidence, and even some courage. It started with a feeling of connection—on my part. We imported many leading (sometimes not-so-leading) health and beauty brands from all over the world into Ireland. My company looked after all the warehousing and distribution, sales and marketing. It was a challenging business (as all businesses are), yet really exciting. The part I enjoyed the most was travelling to conferences and meetings around the world, looking for new "wow" brands, meeting people I wouldn't normally meet, and being in places I wouldn't otherwise be.

Early in 2007, I attended a conference in Monaco and came across a new natural face and body personal care brand called Yes to Carrots. I hadn't heard of it before. I only discovered the brand on the afternoon of the very last day when they were getting ready to pack up and leave. I didn't have an appointment to see them, and they didn't have any availability to make time for me. But I just knew our company would make this brand a success in Ireland. I wanted to do this. This brand had instant high impact and, initially, seemed to tick the boxes of my company's requirements for a new launch. All that remained, from my point of view, was to meet the people behind the brand to see if we connected well and could work together. I've never succeeded with a brand or project where the people involved didn't connect and engage well with one another.

I'm decisive by nature—some would say impulsive—and I made a decision there and then that I would not let this opportunity pass me by. I didn't even have the opportunity, yet, but I still wasn't going to let it pass me by. I mentioned Yes to Carrots to an American colleague at the conference, who had actually met one of the founders of the company at a previous event. I pestered her to introduce me and managed to get a very quick meeting with him and their team just as they were packing up to leave on the final day. I told them about my company, said we'd be a perfect fit, and let them know I really wanted to work with them in Ireland. I remember being so excited about the brand, the products, and the potential for huge success in our market. I later found out that Ireland, where I operated from, wasn't actually on their radar as a launch market—too small.

It took seven months to get them to agree to work with us in Ireland, the longest time it had ever taken my company to reach a deal. I phoned every two to three weeks and emailed in-between calls. After a couple of months, their international representative (reluctantly) agreed to meet with me. I planned for this meeting like never before. The more I worked on the detail of an Irish launch and strategy, the more I believed that this brand would be hugely successful in the market.

The planning was worth it. Because of their timeline (which was slower than my ideal timeline at the time, but which turned out to be for the best), we had time to plan our launch and sales strategy in detail. I invested in quite a lot of inventory, more than ever before with an unknown brand. We immediately made a huge impact with this already impressive brand. Our sales strategy was perfect; PR and promotion worked really well. We even sponsored a big horse racing event and gave the horse a prize of a carrots hamper! We had fun with it. The brand won lots of awards. The result? Net wholesale sales of more than €1.25 million (more than $1.5 million) in the first year of working in a small market. The best part was, this really was a job well done. It wasn't easy, yet the goal was clear, because the brand (and products) was a great one. This gave us the confidence to take action. Interesting, also, was the fact that this success and the learnings from it gave me and my team further confidence in other areas of our work and business. Result!

The Amazing Apollo 13 Team

On a very different note, the saving of the lives of the Apollo 13 crew in April 1970 is one of my favourite examples of an amazing achievement where clarity and confidence contributed hugely to success.

Apollo 13 was the seventh manned mission in the American Apollo space programme and the third intended to land on the Moon. On April 11, 1970, at 13:13 CST, the craft launched from the Kennedy Space Center in Florida. Commander James A. Lovell, Jr., Fred W. Haise, Jr., and Commander John L. "Jack" Swigert were the astronauts on board. Ken Mattingly, originally intentioned to be the third member of the crew, was left behind. Unfortunately, he'd been exposed to German measles and had to be replaced. It was actually a good thing for Apollo 13 that Ken Mattingly was still on the ground. His expertise would soon help save his crewmates.

Immediately following its launch, it seemed as if everything was normal with Apollo 13. But almost fifty-six hours into the flight—at about 10:06 p.m. EST, over 200,000 miles from Earth, on the 13th of April, 1970—Apollo 13 got into serious trouble. The astronauts heard a loud bang, which perhaps was a small meteorite strike or malfunction that had catastrophic consequences for the craft. The astronauts observed a problem with the power supply and the loss of a significant quantity of the oxygen supply held in the storage tanks. After about three minutes, the Supply Module's oxygen supply was entirely depleted. Because the fuel cell depends on the oxygen to generate power, the spacecraft was now entirely dependent on the Command Module's limited-duration battery power and water. The crew was forced to shut down the Command module completely to conserve any power for re-entry—the prospects looked bleak.

The lives of the crew were in serious danger. The severely damaged Service Module had lost its ability to produce electricity, oxygen, and water. Swigert, followed by Lovell, radioed Mission Control the now famous line: "Houston, we've had a problem."

Back in Houston, Mission Control and Ken Mattingly frantically worked together to find a way to get the crew back to Earth. It didn't look hopeful, wasn't easy. The answer to this problem was going to be really complicated.

In the meantime, with their oxygen being depleted, the crew in space had to power down their Command Module ("Odyssey"), power up the Lunar Module ("Aquarius"), and make sure they had working air lines. Aquarius would not take them to the Moon this trip, but thankfully it would help to save their lives.

Solving this problem on the ground meant that flight controllers needed to develop a mission-saving system that could be replicated in space. Simple items, such as cardboard and tape, were used to create what was dubbed "the mailbox," which saved the astronauts. They did it—one hour before re-entry, the crew jettisoned Aquarius. It helped save their lives but would not survive a re-entry.

Apollo 13 landed in the Pacific Ocean 142 hours, 54 minutes, and 41 seconds after lift-off. The USS Iwo Jima recovered the men and Odyssey. Most of this particular mission had occurred under extremely dangerous, life-threatening conditions.

The teamwork between NASA's Houston team and the flight crew members was absolutely brilliant. Connected, clear, calm thinking by Johnson Space Center personnel, working under unbelievable pressure, helped to save the mission and the lives of the crew.

Jim Lovell later said, "I think one of the things that showed the people of the world was that even if there is a great catastrophe, good leadership and teamwork, initiative and perseverance—these things make for getting an almost certain catastrophe into a successful recovery."

Returning the crew safely was one of NASA's finest moments. Without a clear plan, and, more important, the confidence that this plan could be carried out, the Apollo 13 crew would not have survived. If the team did not believe they could save the crew, then they wouldn't have done what was necessary to save their lives. That story always amazes me because it shows the power of the human brain, the resource it is against seemingly insurmountable problems.

When You Try, It's Great to Succeed

As part of my work, and because I am interested in what factors lead to confidence, I recently carried out a confidence survey with forty-seven successful women. Almost 94 percent said they relied on external feedback for confidence. While it's always wonderful to receive positive feedback, indeed necessary to receive feedback from others about how your actions influence the way others perceive you, it's also crucial to listen to your own inner voice. If you don't know who you are and what you're about—and like it—it will be impossible to express your best self to the world and to follow the route that works for YOU.

I realised this on some very tough 600–700 km charity cycles I have done in Europe to raise money for the Irish Hospice Foundation and also when I climbed Mt. Kilimanjaro. It was clear to me that whether someone else thought or said I could do this or not was irrelevant. Only my own mind would decide to overcome the obstacles; only my own legs would get me to the top—nobody else's could do it. I connected with the core of who I was. This was the right task at the right time, with a very clear goal: either it happened or it didn't. I really didn't know whether I could do it or not, whether external factors like the altitude and low oxygen levels would affect the result, whether my training was enough. But one thing for sure, I was going to try.

If you wonder whether you're good enough for the next promotion, would like a different, better life, need to reduce stress, or feel disconnected, as though you're not living the life you know you can live, there's one unavoidable truth: *if you don't take action to change the situation, then the change just isn't going to happen.*

You can nail this. You can finish this book having banished the beliefs and thoughts that are holding you back and with a daily plan of action for you to feel confident and behave confidently. It's okay to feel unconfident and afraid sometimes. Most people do. The good news is that having confidence, setting clear goals, and taking action are skills that can be learned, like everything else, with practice. When you actually do the work (nobody else will do it for you), the potential benefits are huge.

The work starts with the exercises in this book, which will give you deep insight into the following:

1. Who you really are and what you believe about yourself—realizing your value.
2. How smart you are—your strengths (and we'll gather the evidence for these, so there'll be no denying it).
3. What you care about.
4. What your personal best is and how you best operate.

This information about yourself will then help you to do the following:

1. Create your purpose statement and some meaningful, deliverable goals.
2. Design your own Results Catalyst™ formula using tools developed from evidence-based research and also using the information about yourself that you have uncovered by doing the exercises in this book.

Take your time to work through the exercises at the end of most chapters, answer questions honestly, and finish this book having banished the beliefs and thoughts that are holding you back and with a daily plan of action for you to feel confident and behave confidently. You have the power within you to do this, to feel more confident, happy, and successful—connected to who you are.

Why am I so sure this process will work? What evidence is there?

1. It worked for me. I was a pharmacist with a list of achievements. I ran successful businesses, yet I didn't *feel* confident inside. This lack of confidence affected decision making in all areas of my life, especially in business—hiring staff, dealing

with customers/negotiations, employee issues—I would have spent a lot less time dealing with HR issues if I'd had the confidence at the time to do the right thing for the business instead of worrying what the employees and other people would think. I also felt I had to be great at every aspect of the business and didn't ask the right people for help. I followed these steps and Aha! They worked.

2. It has worked for my clients. My Results Catalyst™ system, which I outline in this book, worked for them.
3. And if you'd like further evidence, just read some of the many useful research articles out there until something sparks a connection within you to take action for change.

So, let's challenge your thinking, challenge how you think about successes and failures, how you think about learning from life's lessons, and how confident and happy you want to be. Review your expectations and put any negative beliefs to the test!

Whether you're an astronaut, an entrepreneur, leading a corporate team, running a household, playing sports, climbing mountains—whatever you do, you need to be clear that this is indeed what you want to do and it's essential that you know the steps to take. Confidence, believing that you can do anything, is key to success—nothing will happen without this belief.

In life, how many people at various ages and stages are not where they expected or hoped to be? There may be a clue in the word "hope." Yes, we need hope. In fact, it's an important requirement for happiness and success. But hope alone is not enough. A clear knowledge of what's required, the confidence that the job can be done, a solid plan, and the courage to see it through are all essential elements for success in life and at work.

CHAPTER 2

The Pathway to Success

Success is going from failure to failure without loss of enthusiasm.
—Albert Einstein

Kate was thirty-five, single, and worked in the tech sector as a Web developer. She was so lacking in confidence that she was afraid to have a child, in case she wouldn't be a good mother. She believed she didn't deserve love, but she wasn't sure why. Her mum had never shown her much affection, and Kate wondered whether that was the source of her belief. Or maybe there was another cause. She didn't know. Unworthiness was just a feeling she couldn't shake.

She worked in a competitive business and pushed herself to work long hours so that others with families could get home to their children. She felt that since she was single, with no reason to hurry home in the evenings, she should do the extra work. But after a few years, she began to wonder why she believed she didn't deserve the love and happiness others had. That was when we began to work together. We soon discovered that Kate didn't have a true sense of who she really was, and because of this, she believed she had nothing to offer a partner or a child and wouldn't know how to raise a balanced, happy child who felt loved.

Jack had no confidence, couldn't focus, believed that everyone else was better at their jobs than he was, and felt that all his self-employed friends were more successful than he was with his own business—a retail store he'd owned for ten years. Business was doing okay, but Jack's revenue fell short of where he wanted it to be. Instead of taking steps to increase revenue, he lost focus, and he spent many of his days reading online news and trivia, making no progress, ending every day no better off than when it began. This became a habit he found difficult to break. When he turned forty, he realised how much time he'd wasted and decided to do something about it. I had known Jack for a long time. He'd made some progress with his goals, and when I began coaching him, I asked him if he would try out the Results Catalyst to see if it was helpful and give me his honest feedback.

Even though Jack had made good progress with his business, he wanted to be even more successful. He wasn't getting the results he needed for his company, and that was incredibly stressful for him. Being an entrepreneur, he was responsible for his own financial security, including his pension, and he has a family to support. He wanted to deliver the best results he possibly could.

Michael was terrified of public speaking and sharing his opinions in meetings. Yet as the HR director of a large healthcare business, he had to speak regularly. He spent many sleepless nights and struggled with panic attacks before every presentation. In his role as director, he dealt with a lot of conflict. As his stress levels increased over time, so did his ability to handle conflict, which caused him even further anxiety. It didn't help that he drank at least three strong cups of coffee before each presentation or potentially contentious meeting to steady his nerves. He just got the shakes.

Anna, an accountant in her late twenties, believed she wasn't very likeable, so she refused all social invitations to events where she didn't know people very well, leaving her sometimes feeling lonely. She had a few good friends but found it difficult to connect with new people. She believed that other peoples' opinions mattered more than hers did. Anna worked hard and spent most of her free time alone, which only served to further entrench her negative beliefs about herself. She is a perfectionist and was very hard on herself for every mistake she made. I worked with Anna to help her find the evidence that her negative beliefs were indeed not based on any real truth, to uncover her value system, and to help her realise that she was not alone in her struggles, that others sometimes feel uncomfortable in certain situations too.

When they became my clients, each of these people had varying degrees of success, either running their own business or working at a high level for large companies, yet their own perceived lack of confidence resulted in a ceiling on their success, causing each of them huge anxiety. Kate, deep down, had always wanted to be a mother and felt that time was running out. She cried every time a friend announced her pregnancy, yet she couldn't conquer her feelings of unworthiness. Her own mother had always been very judgemental, which resulted in Kate being supercritical of herself.

Jack valued success and became frustrated during and after his years of inertia when he didn't achieve his goals within his desired timeline—he'd wanted his business to reach €10 million annual sales by the time he turned forty, and he got quite a wake-up call when his birthday came and his business was nowhere near where he'd hoped. Michael and Anna were hyper-concerned about what others thought about them and didn't value themselves; they also had no idea of their strengths and how best to use them to their advantage, either at work or in other areas of their lives.

How could these four find their happiness when it was hidden beneath layers of feelings of inadequacy and the resulting stress? Were they as productive, as successful, as they potentially could be? Of course not. Even though their stories are different, these people had lost connection with themselves, and all of them believed that how others viewed them mattered much more than their own opinions of themselves.

The Results Catalyst—Five Practical Steps to Success

For Kate, Jack, Michael, and Anna, the pathway to success, to banishing these issues, all involved a similar formula—the Results Catalyst. The amount of time each of these four took to get the results they desired varied—from three months to more than a year. However, they all found the courage within to connect to themselves by working through exercises that you'll find in chapter 6:

1. **Gain freedom from limiting, negative, beliefs.** Connect with who you really are and realise your value.

2. **Realise the effectiveness of playing to your strengths.** Know how smart you are by gathering the evidence, so there'll be no denying it.

3. **Live according to your own values, not someone else's.** Do more of what *you* care about.

4. **Formulate your own purpose statement** (*the* greatest tool on earth). This plan will be your guide to help you live and work at your personal best.

5. **DO IT** (Decide, Organise, Implement, Treat). This is a formula for action, for implementing your goals. This step follows naturally from the steps above. You'll read about DO IT in chapter 8.

Our potential, as humans, is amazing. As you work through the exercises for each of these steps, you'll gather the information about yourself that you need to become confident and successful and to get the results you want from life—to live to your potential.

Freedom from Negative Beliefs

There was absolutely no evidence that Kate would be anything other than a great mother. She just had such a huge lack of confidence in her own abilities. She alone believed this about herself—nobody else did. I worked with her to **challenge these negative, limiting beliefs** and replace them with beliefs that were actually true. She now knows that she's a kind and generous person who deserves love and will make a wonderful mother.

Realise Your Strengths

Jack is growing his business and enjoying it a lot more. How? Jack is quick thinking, strategic, and an inspirational leader, who's able to get the best from his team. He came to **appreciate his strengths** and to use these strengths to increase his effectiveness at work. When he and I worked through the steps in the Results Catalyst, he **formulated a very clear purpose statement** for his business and his life, which gives him clarity and helps keep him on track towards his goals. He's aligning with his purpose—always.

Work in Accordance with Your Values

Elvis Presley once said, "Values are like fingerprints. Nobody's are the same, but you leave 'em all over everything you do." I love that quote. And it's so true. Each of us has different values, and it's critical that we understand and align those values, that they inform everything we do.

Michael values a job well done, and in a very short period of time, he realised that because he always prepared so well for his presentations, the content was always excellent. Indeed, because he was so nervous, he always did extra preparation, frequently working late into the night, but he was able to work though his anxiety. He faced his fears and soon started to enjoy speaking up. When Michael came to **remind himself of what he valued** and **appreciate his strengths**—which included attention to detail and clarity in communication—within a matter of weeks, he banished the stress associated with giving presentations and used his new-found energy to perform better in other aspects of his role.

It took some time for Anna to **banish forever the limiting belief** that she wasn't very likeable, just over a year. During that time, she took small action steps. She joined a tennis club, reached out to work colleagues and old friends with whom she'd lost contact, and said yes to invitations. These actions improved her life immediately. Anna had to practice doing what she knew was best for her—living to her own values—for it to become second nature. Through her efforts, she connected with a group of people she knew liked her for who she was. This outer proof further cemented her growing inner conviction that she's a likeable person. I worked with her through the steps listed above. By gaining freedom from her limiting beliefs, she was able to connect with what she valued, finding clarity, confidence, and the courage to conquer her demons. She uncovered the evidence, both internal and external, that she's a lovely, kind person and developed new habits to change her negative thinking patterns to positive ones. Anna is now more generous to others. She's benefitted socially, improved family relationships, and forwarded her career. She's written down her new positive beliefs and reads them whenever she needs a reminder of what's really true about herself. She finds this useful. She now has joy in her life.

Mistakes Are a Great Way to Learn

For me, in business, working through these exercises, finding freedom from my limiting beliefs, and taking decisions that mean I live according to my values, with clarity and a sense of purpose, has made a huge difference in my life. But that doesn't mean working these steps is always easy. Part of the process is being able to take a cold, hard, honest look at where you're at, even if you don't like it. Although I'm happy and relatively successful, I've had my share of embarrassing moments—often in business. Whereas I believe there's always something new to learn in life, since I've carried out the exercises for beliefs, strengths, and values, and formulated my own purpose statement, my "learning experiences" are now not so much the humiliating type. This particular story is a bit embarrassing for me, but I'll tell on myself for the purpose of communicating the lesson.

I once hired someone in a senior management and sales role for my health and beauty sales, marketing, and distribution business. From his first day on the job, he treated the good-looking female staff differently from how he treated the less physically attractive, overweight members. One Friday, he bought chocolate bars for all the ladies in our office—the thin ladies—and told the others "they didn't need them because they were too fat!" I had the sense to reprimand him, and he apologised to those in question, but at the time, I didn't have the clarity (probably dazed from the shock!) or, more likely, the confidence to fire him on the spot. At that point, he'd only been with us for a short time, so we could have easily parted ways. I ignored my intuition, which was actually telling me that I'd made a huge mistake in hiring him in the first place.

Over the course of the next two months, he continued to upset most of my employees, annoy several key customers, and cost the business tens of thousands of euros. Eventually, I was forced to make the decision to let him go. By that time, I had quite a few bridges to mend with employees and customers, and I was hugely embarrassed that I'd allowed all of this to happen. Ouch! This incident was a wake-up call for me to get some clarity on what exactly, within myself, caused me to hire (and often retain others despite warning signs) people whose values were not aligned with those I had for my business. I read books, took a few courses, and started to examine my beliefs and values. I remembered my strengths and got back to using them again!

By following the steps in the Results Catalyst, Kate, Jack, Michael, and Anna gained the clarity and confidence to improve their lives and achieve the results they desired. What if I'd had the clarity of vision and the confidence to make the right decision sooner; that is, what if I hadn't hired such a person in the first place? It was only when I started working on my own beliefs and values, and working to my strengths, that I was able to make better business decisions.

Mistakes happen in life and in business—and with the right attitude, they can actually be valuable learning tools. If you don't decide to learn from your mistakes and change whatever caused them, you'll just keep making the same ones over and over again. Quite early on in my business career, I decided to make a note of what I learned from every such learning experience. First, I stopped using the word "mistake." That alone really helped. I highly recommend it! After my learning experience with the bad hire, I was much clearer about the costs (financial, emotional, reputational) of not connecting to my truth, of not listening to my intuition (there had been earlier signs that I should not have gone ahead with this hire). When I connected to what mattered (when that sales manager and I parted ways), we implemented a more formal hiring process in the company. I employed the services of an experienced interviewer, who consulted with me on a part-time basis, and never again made a hiring decision alone. We always held a minimum of two, sometimes three, interviews and checked references more thoroughly. I also went for interview coaching. Result—I learned new skills and became a more confident recruiter, better at hiring the right people.

Although you can sometimes learn from your mistakes and thus build confidence, it's also important to be proactive and use what you've learned from the experience. The lesson I'd learned about hiring was a hard one for me to learn because I'm impulsive (both a strength and a weakness). I found the hiring process tedious—it was only when I experienced the fallout from not hiring well, and learned from this, that I decided it was far less tedious to put energy into and focus on recruiting well than to rush the process. I actually came to enjoy interviewing.

I used to see myself as an accidental business person, an unintentional entrepreneur. Nothing I did was planned far in advance; I just let it happen. When I started my own business, I had zero business training. Because of my lack of formal business training, I didn't have business confidence, and I trusted other more experienced business people too much. Often I trusted the wrong people; though, thankfully, I often trusted the right ones, too, from whom I learned a lot. I hired the sales manager on the recommendation of someone

I believed in. I didn't make up my own mind. Embarrassing consequences—and costly too! My road to success was a bumpy one.

Formulate Your Own Purpose Statement

Formulating your own purpose statement, as successful businesses do, is an important exercise for creating an invaluable tool. Life before and life after you own your purpose statement is potentially very different. Formulating your purpose statement comes after you are clear on your beliefs and values and when you know your strengths.

Everyone's pathway to success is unique, and that's okay. The basic building blocks for that road, however, are the same for everyone. Give a number of builders the exact same building blocks and other materials to build anything, and each one will work to a different schedule and end up with a different finished product. Connection, clarity, confidence, and conviction are basic building blocks for the results you need in business, in life—completing the steps in the Results Catalyst will give you those building blocks to shape your own success formula and get the results you want.

Throughout the book, as you come to the questions that I ask you to answer honestly, please find somewhere you have space to think, take whatever time you need, and tools to record your thoughts. Use these questions to build a complete picture of who you really are and what success means to you. Working on your answers will be extremely helpful to you when you come to formulate your own purpose statement and design your personal clarity, confidence, and success formula.

CHAPTER 3

Know and Appreciate the Real You

> *The one unforgivable sin in any society.*
> *Be different and be damned!*
> —Margaret Mitchell, *Gone with the Wind*

When I first met Jeanette at a business dinner, she came across as doing really well for herself. She was bright, bubbly, and happy on the outside. Yet she was a little brittle. She was a very successful lawyer with a major firm, looked fit and healthy, and had two lovely children—an eight-year-old son and a ten-year-old daughter. Jeannette smiled a lot, and she presented herself as being on top of the world and happy with life.

When I really got to know Jeanette as a client, she said that balancing all areas of her life was virtually impossible. Just being able to race home to kiss the kids goodnight was often difficult—and she felt so guilty about not spending more time with them. She felt under huge pressure to deliver at work, often working twelve-to-fourteen-hour days to get the job done. She enjoyed her work but it was draining her; it used up all her resources. She hardly ever spent time with her kids, and at weekends, she was so tired after her week's work that she wasn't at her best. In fact, her husband and children saw the absolute worst side of her—the impatient, controlling side, the side that snapped at her husband when he didn't put the dishes in the correct place in the dishwasher!

Jeannette told me that she and her husband were having problems communicating. When she started seeing me, they were hardly speaking to one another at all. She'd had fertility issues before her children were born—they were both conceived via in-vitro fertilization (IVF). The IVF treatments had taken so much out of her both physically and emotionally. Her husband had found it really stressful too. To be honest, she said, her relationship with her husband had never recovered from those terrible years. The recession started when she had thought her relationship with her husband was at an all-time low. And then it got even worse.

Jeannette and her husband had been to couples counselling, which, in her words, "had put a BAND-AID" over the problems, but they hadn't continued the counselling for as long as they needed to. Recently, things between them had gotten a little better, but they weren't as good as Jeannette would've liked them to be—not what her hopes and dreams were made of. She longed to recapture some of the feelings they'd had for each other at the start of their marriage. She missed the way they used to chat for hours every evening over a nice dinner and a bottle of wine and spend the weekends outdoors, climbing, cycling, and catching up with friends. And laugh. She missed the way they used to laugh together.

In other areas of her life, Jeanette also felt that things could be better. She exercised, usually walking to work and using the gym at her office. But she hadn't time to see her friends or her extended family. She never read anything that wasn't work related. She'd stopped sleeping, waking up feeling anxious at 3:00 a.m. almost every morning, after which she couldn't get back to sleep, and often ended up going to work well before 5:00 a.m. She'd started to have some health issues—headaches, heartburn, stomach aches. And she worried all the time.

Jeanette is an amazing woman. When she came to see me, she was prepared to dig deep to find out what she really wanted from life. She was also prepared to do what it took to live her best life. She'd realised she could do better in all areas of her life, but because she was overwhelmed with responsibilities, she'd lost the confidence to make the changes needed. She was totally disconnected from who she really was, the person she'd been "before," and the person she knew she really was.

Because Jeannette actually recognised the disconnect, she was off to a good start. She decided she was ready for change and wanted to provide herself with the tools to make the right changes. She needed help. She was concerned that there was so much wrong in her life that it would take huge measures to "fix it." She blamed herself for everything that had gone wrong, and she'd stopped showing herself the kindnesses she deserved. Jeanette had lost confidence in her abilities as a wife and mother. She wasn't happy. She knew she wasn't living her best life, and she needed help to know what to do and where to start. She had decided to take action.

Make Room for Joy

A story like Jeanette's is not that unusual. As we get older, with increased responsibilities and capacity for worry, life gets busier, more intense. Jeanette also had a mum in her nineties who was unwell, and her husband's parents, while doing okay, were in their eighties and needed to be looked after too. Jeanette's is actually a familiar story, and I ask you, where is the room for connection to self, fun, joy, even contentment when life is so pressured? Where does someone like Jeanette start in the process of regaining confidence?

The starting point is to get to know the real you and then to appreciate and love this person. Embrace who you are. It's okay to be you. In fact, it's great to be you. Stop pretending to be someone else. When you're aware of your capabilities (and also areas of weakness), you know your value. Even with a life as busy and overwhelming as Jeanette's, there's room for fun and joy. It's absolutely necessary to find joy in your life, especially during stressful periods. You just need to make the decision to spend time looking for it, recognising it, and cultivating it. It's natural that life has its ups and downs. There will be busy periods and times of stress. Finding moments of joy and knowing how to have fun, actually having fun, can help you navigate the stressful times, remain focused, and be happier and more successful in life.

I can tell you, there are times in my life when I have to work at finding the joy, but the things I love are being outdoors—even in the rain—having dark chocolate, and most important, getting a big hug from my daughter. I make sure to fit the things that bring me joy into the most stressful periods. When business colleagues from all over the world used to visit Ireland, we often took the time to find joy by working at a little-known picnic spot near our office with a magnificent view, overlooking a lake in the mountains (except when it was raining).

Your life may not have the issues that Jeanette's had. But are you 100 percent happy with where you are? Is there something you'd like to do more of but lack the confidence to get started doing? Something you'd like to be better at? Are you looking for a promotion at work? Do you feel you're living life to please others, yet not doing a great job of it because you're disconnected from yourself and not feeling positive or happy? It doesn't have to be a huge change you're after, although maybe it is. That change can be as small as exercising an extra hour every week or cutting down your caffeine intake. Or that change may be bigger, like going for a promotion at work. Ask the questions and answer honestly. For most of us (it's human nature), there are some habits we'd like to swap for other habits that would serve us better in life, habits that would help us have the best life-experience possible. I often swap exercise for TV; Jeannette got into the habit of meditating. What habit can you change to serve you better?

Where will you look to find your own connection, your clarity, confidence, and the results you need? Is there anything new that can help you? I believe that we all have our own unique way of living our best life. Different habits will work for different people. Some "gurus" will tell you never to check your email first thing in the morning because you're wasting your most productive hours. Others will say that it's best to check your email early, deal with it, and get on with your day. Another guru will tell you to ditch emails altogether. You can't listen to all of them, right? You need to choose what works for you. However, that said, there are some actions and habits that serve us well in the quest for confidence, happiness, and success. There are some basic formulas you can adopt for your own life to deliver what you need. You'll find these later on in this book in chapters 6 and 8.

Celebrate Your Uniqueness

Whether you like it or not, we're all unique. Yet, in our society, there can be huge pressure to be like others, which starts at a very early age. And the quest to be like others can hugely undermine confidence. At some level, we like to be different. While it may be flattering when a friend copies your style, house décor, type of car, or whatever, if you turn up at an event in the same dress as someone else, it really doesn't feel good.

Knowing and appreciating the real you starts with believing in yourself, believing that you deserve to be confident, happy, successful, and deserve to live your best life. If a son, daughter, or other loved one was living your life, doing the things you do, would you be happy for them? Remember—you're as deserving of love as everyone else. Achievement is not necessary for you to deserve love. When you realise that and actually believe it in your soul, you'll release the ties that are holding you back.

When Jeanette began the process of getting to know herself, connecting with who she really was, and believing that she was enough, she realised that, deep down, she hadn't been loving herself, hadn't been kind to herself, and was actually starting to exhibit martyr tendencies, which her husband and family absolutely hated, and which served no purpose for herself either.

Crucial to Jeanette's success is that she took action to make the changes she needed, which gave her the results she wanted. She explored her beliefs about herself and realised that, deep down, she believed that if she didn't achieve success in everything she did, then she didn't deserve to be happy, that she had to earn happiness and respect. When she thought about her values, she came to know that her family was the most important aspect of her life. She also valued her career but not at the current cost to her family. She reminded herself of what her strengths were (openness, kindness, creativity, quick-thinking, capable). And even though her family was incredibly important to her, her behaviour on a daily basis wasn't communicating that to anyone. That particular disconnect between her values and her actions caused her much anxiety. So she formulated her own purpose statement (which you will also be guided towards doing later in chapter 6). She was then ready to take action.

To get started on reconnecting to who you really are and what you want in life, get paper and something to write with, find a quiet spot, answer the following questions honestly, and complete the lists. I recommend getting a notebook to record your answers to the exercises in this book. You'll return to them often to review and update, so it comes in handy when you have all your work in one place.

Are You Living Your Best Life?

Is your life a life that's lived as being true to you, acknowledging who you really are, and realising what's important to you?

Exercise 1

List three examples of times during the last year where you were truly happy and connected. Complete the picture for each one: Where were you? What were you doing? Who were you with? What did it feel like? Was there a fragrance associated with the experience that reminds you of that wonderful time, a taste? Answer every question in detail.

1. List three things that that make you unhappy at this moment. Is your weight bothering you? Your boss? Complete the picture again: Where are you? What are you doing? Who are you with (or are you alone)? What does the experience feel like? Smell like? Taste like? Describe everything in detail.
2. What exactly is missing in your life? Write down the ingredients you don't have in your life that you wish you had.
3. What precisely is stopping you? List the barriers to your success.
4. What actions do you think someone who's unstoppable in the pursuit of their dreams would take?

The goal of this book is to act as a catalyst to help you get the results you want in life. The processes and exercises will help you to connect with who you really are and what exactly it is you want—not what anybody else wants for you. Save all the answers to the questions as you go along. This information will help you take those positive steps towards turning your life around.

CHAPTER 4

Find the Evidence—The Positives for Positivity

If you think you can do a thing or think you can't do a thing, you're right.
—Henry Ford

When my wholesale distribution business started dealing with key buyers for major retailers in our industry, I was a bit scared. At the time, I had zero experience meeting and dealing with key buyers, and I really didn't know what to expect. After the first few meetings, it became clear to me that preparation, clear objectives, and a positive mindset were critical to coming to a mutually beneficial agreement every time. Before each meeting, I set my intention that each side would be happy with the outcome. As President Obama said in his 2009 inauguration speech, "On this day, we gather because we have chosen hope over fear, unity of purpose over conflict and discord." Now, he had bigger issues to deal with than retailer meetings! But each person's dreams are important to him or her, and if you don't have hope and optimism that you'll achieve your life's goals, then you're putting yourself at a huge disadvantage, to say the very least.

Positive Attitudes—Higher Sales

In my various businesses, I led and managed sales teams. With most of the team members, it was very clear when they were happy. When life was going well, they absolutely smashed those sales targets. But when things went wrong, many of them couldn't focus on sales—they couldn't find enough positivity to reach the goals we'd set. I remember a few people, though, who no matter what life threw at them, could always see a positive side. These were the people who were loved by our customers and other employees, and they consistently reached their personal and professional goals. Indeed, I myself looked forward to seeing these people every day, and I learned a lot from them.

What these employees had in common was that they knew who they were. They knew their strengths and what they valued. They asked for help when they needed it, and the rest of the time, they knew how to use their strengths to get results. Knowing what you're best at and what you value gives you the clarity you need to make informed decisions. When I had my wholesale business, I had the pleasure of working with a key account person who really valued customer relationships. She knew that building trusted relationships with people was her key strength. She was also good with numbers and paid attention to detail, both of which really helped in sales. The customer always came first with her, and she would never do anything to jeopardise a customer relationship. In fact, she went out of her way to help. Because treating customers aligned with three of her key values—honesty, trust, and relationships—and she was able to draw on her strengths, thus bringing clarity to her work, she consistently delivered for our customers and for the company.

Many people think they have no time in their life to think about values and strengths and that sort of stuff—it's too fluffy for them. They believe only wimps think about confidence, happiness, connecting to the person within, and finding "me" time in a busy world. These people just keep on going—working hard, playing hard, always busy, surviving on four or five hours sleep most nights. I know people who have this attitude. While there's an argument for just getting on with it and not overthinking, it's crucial that when you do actually take action towards goals, you're working on the right ones; you're starting from a place of connection, clarity, and total engagement. That said, when you get to chapter 6, you want to approach the exercise with a positive mindset, so you're totally engaged in each step of the exercises and your life.

We Have More Potential Than We Realise

Wouldn't it be amazing to get the results you want in life with less stress and while engaging daily with what matters to you—living with connection, energy, joy, and confidence.

In his blog in *The Huffington Post*, Eldon Taylor asks, "What Constitutes an Authentic Life?" He quotes five notable authors and philosophers, including Tolstoy, Gandhi, and Nietzsche, and comes to his own conclusion that it is "the mindful life, aware and engaged in our inner most self-discovery, alert to the fact that as we live, we literally live into who we are—or we don't…"

Connecting to yourself, maintaining positive habits, and searching for your inner joy—all of which result in increased confidence—are absolutely necessary for you to reach your potential. Studies show that happiness breeds success, and that optimism and positivity are good for your health, well-being, career, and business results.

Science proves that optimism and positivity lead to success and a more fulfilled, happier life. Most people know that, but what happens when you just don't feel positive, and you can't seem to grab hold of those happy, engaged, connected feelings. Sometimes, hearing about other people's positivity can actually reinforce the stress regarding why you can't be like that, so-why not try to look at it another way? Why not learn the lessons from how they stay upbeat and live their best lives?

Positivity—To Help with Challenges

While positive attitudes and stories can increase our own positivity, mistakes are a different story. We don't learn from the mistakes of others; we learn from our own. When the recession hit in 2008, and my company, like every other, was challenged with survival, I went through a couple of weeks of feeling sorry for myself and thinking, "Just when we were on a roll, when things had been going well, this happens." I really wanted out. But I couldn't just "get out." I sought help from a trusted advisor, who gave me a pep-talk (I will always remember that conversation), in which he told me exactly what I needed to do and reminded me to keep a positive outlook. "After all," he said, "you don't have a choice if you want your company to survive and prosper. So looking at this positively will benefit you and everyone in the company. This time will pass either way." He was someone whose advice I valued, so I decided to take his advice about being positive. It worked. Those few years during the recession weren't easy, but we survived and even managed to have some fun along the way. I had to search a bit to find things to be positive about, but I did it. It's important for each one of us to uncover the evidence from our own lives that when we're positive, results are better.

Your Personal Evidence for Positivity Worksheet

Complete the exercises below to create a tool to remind yourself of the times when you felt positive. You'll need a notebook and something to write with. Answer the questions, keep the information to hand, and review it when you need something to grab hold of positive feelings.

Exercise 2

1. Describe a time when you felt on top of the world—the absolute best time you can remember in your life. Dig deep for the feelings you had back then, even if it was a very long time ago. Give yourself time to remember and indulge in the feelings associated with this wonderful time. As with the previous exercise in chapter 3, where you listed three happy times in the past year, complete the picture. Where were you? What were you doing? Who were you with? What did it feel like? Is there a fragrance associated with that wonderful time that triggers the memory? A taste? Describe everything in detail now. Remember it. Feel those feelings once again.

2. Still gathering evidence, ask yourself what brings you joy. Real, true, unadulterated joy. Is it when you're with family, friends, running in the outdoors, climbing mountains, practising yoga, listening to birds singing? Whatever it is, you must be honest about it here.

3. Think of an example at work and a second one in your family life where you handled a stressful situation really well because you decided to be positive and optimistic

about the outcome, where you got the results you wanted. How did that feel?

4. Can you think of any situation that you handled well and got the result you wanted when you were feeling negative, pessimistic? Hmm, really?

5. I know that when I don't exercise most mornings I begin to feel lethargic and sometimes a little sad. It just takes a thirty-minute run to change those feelings towards the positive, so I've trained myself to either take a class or brave the elements (most mornings) and get outside and walk or run. How can you use your mornings to suit *you* best, so that the rest of your day is better, more productive? Write down now the tasks you need to do during the first two hours of your day to maximise your success for the rest of the day. Also, list the benefits of doing this for yourself.

It's crucial that as you get closer to doing that all-important work on your beliefs, strengths, values, and purpose in chapter 6, you approach that work with the hope and optimism that you will succeed. Your positive mindset will benefit you hugely in working towards the results you want in life.

CHAPTER 5

What on Earth's Stopping You?

*The smallest of actions is always better than
the noblest of intentions.*
—Robin Sharma, author and leadership speaker

Do you know people who complain about the same problems over, and over again, yet do absolutely nothing about them? Are you one of those people? To a certain extent, we are all that person. Well, nothing about your life will change unless you do something about it. That may sound harsh, but wishing some particular challenge away won't make it so. I know. I used to wish I had a different career, but nothing changed for me until I actually took action.

When I owned and managed my retail pharmacy business, I loved certain aspects of the business, like meeting customers and hearing their (sometimes funny, often heart-breaking) stories; buying and selling aromatherapy, skincare, and colour cosmetics; merchandising to maximise the shopping experience and sales; and organising in-store promotions and events. But I really didn't like the fact that, as a retail pharmacist with my own business, my workday took place inside a small room with no option to pop outside for a short walk or even a quick coffee. I felt as if life were happening outside the confines of the store, especially as the pharmacy section was at the very back with no windows. I would have needed a relief pharmacist to take over for me to have a break, which was possible to get for a day at a time, but not for an hour.

I complained about my situation (quite a lot) to anyone who would listen. But what was stopping me from making a change? Looking back, what stopped me from making changes was the fact that I didn't have clarity about what options were open to me or what else I was capable of. I was also a little afraid of the unknown. I was lucky that the opportunity arose to sell my business—and I made the decision to make the most of that opportunity—but I didn't do the deep and meaningful work on myself, starting with examining my beliefs and values, until years later.

Jeanette, who I introduced in chapter 3, had been afraid for a long time to do something about improving her life. She believed it was selfish to put her energy into her own confidence and happiness. She also felt she should just get on with things, and on some level, she was afraid of the upheaval change might bring. But finally, she realised that doing nothing was having a detrimental effect on her well-being, happiness, and success and that not making changes, and living the way she was living, was much worse than any potential change could be. That realisation galvanised her into action.

On a lighter note, how about that holiday you want to take, that mountain you'd like to climb, that massage you know you need, that friend you'd love to catch up with but can't seem to get around to?

What's stopping you? How do *you* get in your own way?

Starting Small Can Result in Big Changes

The thing is, people often think they need to make really big changes to create any impact—not true at all. It's about making the right changes, often not as big as they seem. Fear is what usually stops many of us from making changes that, deep down, we know we need to make for our lives to be happier and more successful. This fear can be hidden under a façade of bravado or pretence that everything is okay. It's very basic stuff, like knowing your value and purpose in life, that's required to increase confidence and happiness levels, yet this "stuff" requires you to study it and to act on it, to decide every day that you believe in yourself and you will act according to what's important to you.

Start with even one belief: act on one value. If you value your family and don't have much time with them due to work commitments, make sure the time you spend together is great. I would suggest that trying the process of examining your beliefs, reminding yourself of your strengths and values, formulating your own purpose statement, and then using this information about yourself to get the results you want is the best place to start. Confidence, health, and happiness are not luxuries in life, but the bare necessities for success and living at your very best.

Nobody else will do it for you. Who's responsible? You!

In previous chapters, you had the opportunity to remind yourself of instances where you were at your happiest and what brings you joy. In chapter 3, did you answer the questions on what's stopping you and what would someone who's unstoppable do?

If you answered these, please revisit your answers now. Have you answered honestly and completely? At this stage, is there anything else you would like to add?

Gathering Your Own Evidence

You can ask yourself the questions in this section on a daily basis to delve further into what's happening in your life that's preventing you from reaching your goals and living your dreams. Answer the questions below to evaluate where you are and to get started on the process of making changes for better results. You'll need your notebook and something to write with. Once more, I recommend giving yourself enough time to think about your answers and to work from a calm space in which you feel comfortable.

Exercise 3

1. What about my life isn't the way I want it to be?
2. List the three most important reasons why I think this is the way it is.
3. Do I have days when I just don't focus?
4. How many days? Add these up to calculate how many days per year. (When I added up these numbers some years ago, I was shocked at the answer. I wouldn't like to tell you how many hours and days I didn't perform even remotely at my best. The number focused me—I hope it will do the same for you.)
5. Is there a pattern to these days? Describe the pattern.
6. Do I have days when I achieve a lot?
7. How many days?
8. Is there a pattern to these days? Describe the pattern.
9. What has happened in the past forty-eight hours to cause me to procrastinate on an important task?
10. What have I done in the past week that has held me back?

11. What have I not done in the past week that would have moved me further towards my goals?
12. How does that make me feel right now?
13. What *should* I do?
14. What are the top three actions I can take immediately to change how I feel and get results?
15. What will happen if I make these changes?
16. How will I feel if I make the changes? (Describe in detail what you will see, hear, taste, and feel when you take the actions you listed in Question 14.)
17. How will I feel if I don't make the changes?
18. What will happen if I don't make the changes?
19. Am I going to make these changes?
20. When will I take action?

The next set of questions is designed to remind you of what exactly helps you laugh and smile. It's amazing how often people forget to include laughter and relaxation in their lives. A reminder every now and then, followed by action (including these instances in your daily life), can be a great starting point for your pathway towards success.

Exercise 4

1. Do you believe you would be happier if you raised the bar on your performance in any area of your life? If you reached your potential?
2. What passionately drives you?
3. Do you laugh every day? When you laugh, what makes you laugh?

4. Do you smile every day? What makes you smile?
5. Do you have a period every day when you feel relaxed? What relaxes you?

Now, in the spirit of nothing-will-change-unless-you act-differently, having answered all the questions above, what's the one thing you can do today (it doesn't have to be a big thing, just something to get you started) that will change your life for the better, right now?

Having the answers to these questions will help you do the work on your beliefs, strengths, and values in chapter 6, which is crucial for connection, clarity, and confidence, and for helping you make the changes you need to get the results you want. Do it—for you.

CHAPTER 6

Results Catalyst—The Formula for Freedom Beckons

Our beliefs become our thoughts. Our thoughts become our words. Our words become our habits. Our habits become our values. Our values become our destiny.
—*Gandhi*

Angelina Jolie once made a speech that really impressed me. She spoke about how lucky she was to be able to live the life she does, a life with meaning and that which makes a difference, while somewhere else in the world, possibly in a refugee camp, lives another woman with the same intelligence and skill set, the same abilities, and who is maybe even more accomplished at acting in movies and making speeches, yet doesn't have the opportunities to effect change. Angelina Jolie is indeed lucky, lives her best life, uses her talents to the best of her ability, and has made a positive difference in the world for so many people.

Do you want to live your best life? Most people do. Doesn't it feel fantastic when someone tells you or shows you that you've helped them and made a difference? Wouldn't the world be a much better place if each one of us decided to show kindness to even one or two people on a regular basis? Yet to be at your personal best, you need to know what that personal best actually is. Sometimes life can be so busy that it's easy to forget what we're great at—there never seems to be enough time to think. Often people believe it's selfish to devote time to personal awareness and self-development. Really, though, everyone's world is a better place when surrounded by people who are empathic, happy, kind, generous, fun—living their best lives.

To achieve your personal best, you need to believe it's possible. To start to live your best life, those negative, limiting beliefs must absolutely be banished from your mind. This is the stage in the book where your real work begins. It's time to write down what you actually believe about yourself and analyse how believing what you do works for you—or not.

Freedom from Limiting Beliefs

How do you change the way you have always thought about yourself—your long-held beliefs? First, acknowledge what you believe. Be honest with yourself, as this is the quickest way to change those beliefs that aren't working for you. Remember—very small changes can deliver big results. Changing your beliefs about reality is a powerful way to change the reality that you experience, because what you believe to be true is what you create to be true. For Kate, who used to believe she wasn't good enough to deserve the love of a child in her life, working through these exercises helped her free herself from that negative belief that felt like, to use her own words, "chains being unlocked from my heart." Banishing her negative beliefs about herself opened up a whole world of possibilities for her.

When I started coaching, a negative belief wormed its way into my system. I believed that I couldn't possibly be a great coach without hundreds of hours of experience. Given that I had been through the process of analysing my beliefs, knowing my strengths, values, and purpose, I quickly substituted this negative belief with "I am a great coach who delivers the results for my clients that they desire." I prepared (over-prepared) for each client meeting and, hey presto, my very first client referred two new clients within a very short time. If I hadn't substituted the negative belief for a positive one, I may never have had that one client in the first place.

The following exercises will help you make the changes you need to get the results you want. Take whatever time you need to answer the questions in this chapter and the rest of the book, so you can find the answers that you really connect with. You'll want to get your notebook and something to write with and find a quiet place to do these exercises.

How does what you believe about yourself work for you?

This exercise will help you determine your limiting beliefs and replace them with positive ones.

Exercise 5.

1. What are the biggest problems or issues you face in achieving your goals and desires?

2. Identify three deep-rooted beliefs that may be limiting you, that is, that contribute most to the issues. For example, do you believe you don't deserve love, happiness, or success? Do you believe you're not likeable? Do you believe that unless you work longer than everyone else you don't deserve to succeed? Do you believe you're not good enough, that failure is humiliating? What do you believe about yourself that holds you back? Write down three negative beliefs you have about

yourself that are causing the problems you identified in Question 1, the ones that interfere most with your goals. Be honest.

3. We all choose how we behave and are also free to choose what we believe about ourselves and the world. For each of your three negative beliefs listed above, identify what you would need to believe to be true for each one, for you to change them from holding you back to helping you get what you want? For example, if you believe that failure is only bad, substituting that belief with, "Failure is a learning experience and makes me stronger" or even "Failure gives me funny stories to tell" is much more useful and can help you make that essential change to get what you want. I'm guessing that if you believe you must work harder than everyone else to succeed, you probably spend more time in the office than everyone else, to the detriment of other areas of your life—right? Swapping this belief for something like, "I am productive and deliver my work on time" can actually help you do just that. They're your beliefs, so use your own words to formulate your new set of positive ones.

To embed the new beliefs in your being, to really feel that new belief, it's crucial that you actually believe it. There are a number of ways that help to do this:

1. Focus on these positive beliefs daily. Repeat them every day as positive affirmations. For example, "I am great at interviews" and "I am kind and loveable."
2. Write down these beliefs and then read them every day.
3. Visualise yourself as whatever you believe. For example, if you would like to be a powerful public speaker, imagine yourself on that stage, speaking to an enthralled crowd, to huge applause.

4. Test the new beliefs. For example, if you now believe you're productive at work, give yourself the task of getting your work finished by 5:00 p.m., feeling good about it, and getting out of your workplace to have some fun.

Choose the method of embedding these beliefs that works best for you. You may choose more than one.

Realise the Effectiveness of Playing to Your Strengths

One of my favourite books in the coaching and leadership genre is *Strengths Finder 2.0* by Tom Rath. In his book, he writes, "People have several times more potential for growth when they invest energy in developing their strengths rather than their deficiencies." For example, I know that I'm no good at (and have zero interest in) resolving any technology issue from a computer that freezes or a phone that "seems" to lose all its data. So I always ask my husband to look after these tasks. The problem is usually fixed within a couple of minutes. But it used to be difficult for me to ask him for help; I've always believed that just because I'm female, it doesn't mean I can't do anything I want to, so early in my marriage, I tried to prove I could do everything. I often tried to fix computers, unblock drains, and move heavy furniture, which wasted time because my husband was better at these tasks, and he could deal with them in no time. Besides, I ended up asking him for help anyway. But when I took inventory of my strengths, I realised that because these tasks are easier for him, it was much more efficient for the household if he does them. One of my strengths is organising, so I deal with most of the organising for our family organisational issues including our daughter's schedule. This works for us, and we are working to our strengths.

Often it helps to remind yourself what exactly your strengths are. The following exercise will help you do that.

Exercise 6

1. In chapter 4, we did an exercise where you listed a time when you felt on top of the world. Now, list two more times in your life or at work where you felt on top of the world, when you achieved your goals and truly believed in yourself. Remember in detail the circumstances of each event.

Ask yourself the following questions about each of those times:

- What were you doing?
- Were you with other people?
- If so, who were you with?
- What need or desire was fulfilled for you?
- How and why did the experience give your life meaning?
- What other factors contributed to that great feeling?
- Which of your own strengths contributed to this success? (The Evidence)

2. Using your answers from the above exercise, plus your answers to the same exercise you performed in chapter 4, list your strengths.

Work to Your Values

Imagine a life where you could spend your time, at work and outside of work, doing what you most enjoy, doing things that matter to you. Understanding what you value most in life is an essential tool for helping make wise choices and is crucial for happiness, joy, and success.

Here are some examples of values: ability, independence, creativity, family, friendship, integrity, laughter, helping, balance, empathy, decisiveness, fairness, success, respect, leadership, excitement, courage, trust, service, resilience, clarity, wisdom, calmness, acceptance, courage, beauty, forgiveness, influence, health, and altruism.

To complete this exercise, answer the questions below.

Exercise 6.1

1. What's important to you? What really matters to you?
2. It helps to run through your daily and weekly actions and ask yourself: "How do I feel when I do or don't behave in a certain way? What makes me feel happy, sad, tired, energetic, positive, generous? How will I feel if I do or don't exercise? How do I feel if I choose to skip that party at a friend's place? How will I feel if I rush that presentation rather than focus for an hour or two and prepare?"

Completing the exercise above, without judgement, helps lead you naturally to the realisation of your own personal values. When we're crystal clear about what we value most in life, then we have in our hearts what we need to define our sense of purpose. Clarity about what you value is essential to developing achievable goals. And achievable goals are crucial to getting the results you want.

Fulfilled, successful people (in life and in business) are those who have a clearly defined purpose. Confident people have a purpose, and people with a purpose are confident.

Once we know ourselves and what we value, the next step towards revealing to ourselves our true purpose is to take a look at how our daily actions reflect what we value. The accumulation of our beliefs, experiences, and actions shape who we are. Greatness and reaching our potential come when our actions mirror our values. It's easy to trot out "family" as a value. However, if family is a core value, but work or other pursuits leave you with no time or energy for family in your life, then there's discord between what you value and honouring those values. I believe that "where there's a will, there's a way" and that when we're clear about what we really value, then putting some thought into how to act in accordance with what we value, and following through, pays dividends in the results we're able to achieve.

How many people do you know who value success? Yet many don't look after their energy levels, don't get adequate sleep, and don't live a healthier lifestyle to give themselves the stamina and clarity of thought to reach their full potential at work.

To help you measure whether you currently live your life according to what matters to you, fill in the table below to see how you're honouring your values. For example, if you value creativity, does your current role provide you with opportunity for creative expression? If you value independence, do the people you've chosen to surround yourself in life accept this aspect of you?

Exercise 7

Value	Level of Honouring (1-10)

The Magic Ingredient: Create Your Own Purpose Statement

In business, how much time and money is wasted when there's no clear purpose for a meeting, an event, a new product, or a marketing and advertising campaign? In your life, do you waste time participating in various activities, or not act at all because you lack a clear purpose?

Oprah Winfrey wanted to be a teacher. Her purpose: "to be known for inspiring my students to be more than they thought they could be." While her medium ended up being TV rather than the classroom, I think we're all aware of how many people Oprah has inspired in her life. Oprah had a clearly defined purpose, and she honoured it. "I believe there's a calling for all of us," Oprah writes on her website. "I know that every human being has value and purpose. The real work of our lives is to become aware. And awakened. To answer the call."

A 2014 study from Deloitte verifies that organisations that focus their energies on more than sheer profit do better than those without a "culture of purpose."

Increasingly, people, especially younger people, are seeking to join organisations with values and a purpose that are aligned with their own. Companies that clearly communicate their own values and sense of purpose are better positioned to hire employees who share those values, thus creating stronger, more cooperative teams, working more efficiently towards success.

It's not just enough to pay lip service to a culture of purpose. Actions must follow. Each of us can benefit hugely by deciding what our own purpose is and by doing our absolute best to live to it.

At this stage in the book, if you've completed the various exercises, you are well placed to begin formulating your very own purpose statement.

"Purpose" is defined as the reason that something exists: the reason for doing something that gives meaning to actions. Purpose is unique and personal. We don't measure it, yet it hugely influences goals we measure all the time. Purpose is *felt* in your heart.

My personal purpose statement is as follows: "I am the best mum I can be to my daughter, Holly; I make wise health choices; and I am successful in a career I love, while helping as many people as I can along the way."

Reminding myself of the different elements of my purpose statement helps in all areas of my life. For example, if I'm going to help as many people as I can while building a successful career, I need to constantly learn and develop my coaching and training skills, which means reading a coaching journal instead of watching an episode of *Nashville* on TV! Another area where I have found my purpose statement useful is working around nutrition and meals. I'm not such a wonderful cook and get fed up dishing out the same old dinners day after day, week after week, month after month, especially to an eleven-year-old and her friends who say, "not this again," yet won't eat anything else. Often it would be easier not to bother convincing them to eat the broccoli or tomatoes and say "yes" to toast and chocolate cake. In fact, it would *always* be easier! But, when I refer to my purpose statement, the part about doing the best for my daughter, I cook the dinner (again), and she eats her broccoli (again). I hope she'll come to know the wisdom of eating well in future years, and if she doesn't, then at least she will have had a reasonably healthy start in life.

Also, when I'm having days where it's difficult to focus, I see this statement (written on a page on my desk) and realise that I won't make a success of any career unless I do something about it. That statement helps keep me more consistent than I would be otherwise. Not at all perfect, just a lot more consistent.

Consider your new beliefs, strengths, and values to put together your purpose statement. Give yourself time and space to feel your statement. It may need a few tweaks here and there until it feels absolutely right for you. Believe me—the time you spend on your statement is worth it.

Now You Have the Tools to Set New, Realisable Goals

Many of us create mental, verbal, and often written goals to work towards in adult life—both personal and career goals. Where my own goals are concerned, I've achieved many (selling my pharmacies, climbing various mountains, finally being able to do a proper backbend in yoga), but many I haven't (climbing other mountains, visiting Antarctica and Bhutan, and learning a funny poem or Irish dance, so I have a party piece when called upon). While it's always quite satisfactory to cross an achieved goal off a list, the feeling I had in the past was often more a sense of relief than exhilaration. In 2013, I reviewed in detail the lists of goals I'd set over the years, and I realised that some of my goals weren't the right ones (to live in New York, or Nashville—I love American country music and Elvis); others were unrealistic (climbing Mt. Everest), while with different goals (to launch my own skincare brand), fear of failure held me back, and by the time I had dealt with that fear, the timing wasn't right anymore. I became frustrated looking at the various lists and not being able to draw that satisfactory line through the written goals.

When I truly examined my feelings about the goals I hadn't achieved, I realised that because I hadn't examined my beliefs about myself, reminded myself about what I valued (because I was too busy), and remembered my strengths (I can organise anything, and I'm creative and determined), my goals had no purpose; they weren't always the right goals—the ones I really wanted to achieve. Aha! Everything fell into place. It seemed so simple. How could I have not known this? Was I stupid or what? Did everyone else know? When I did the work (on beliefs, strengths, and values) and formulated my own purpose statement, the goals I set felt right, and I started to enjoy the feeling of crossing an achieved goal off my list. Of course, I haven't achieved every single goal—not by a long shot (I still haven't been to Bhutan, Newfoundland, or Antarctica or had the opportunity to meet Oprah), but the percentage of the goals I've achieved has increased, and I'm a lot happier with that number.

Do any of your goals feel like something you "should do," rather than something you dream of achieving? Have you asked yourself (and answered honestly) how you will feel when you achieve these goals? Goals can be an ego trip (I think this was partly the case with my Mt. Everest goal—it sounded great!). While having goals is an important step towards getting things done, I don't believe it's the first place we should start when planning life, happiness, and reaching our full potential in our personal and professional lives. Pursuing goals without meaning is just a waste of energy. Goals are wonderful—achievable with less stress and more meaningful—when backed by clear values and a sense of purpose.

Now that you're armed with a set of positive beliefs, you're clear on your strengths and values, and you've written a purpose statement that you connect with, you'll want to set goals. Copy the table below into your notebook, and then write down the goals that feel right to you.

Exercise 8

	Goals	What will achieving this goal mean to me/my business?	What are the first three steps I need to take to achieve this goal?	Date to achieve?
1				
2				
3				

It's advisable to develop goals in more than one area of your life. I suggest writing your goals in the positive instead of the negative; that is, "I am developing a healthy cash flow, with x (your required amount) of cash availability each month." Write down each goal in detail as shown in the example above. While smaller goals are great, you'll want to also think BIG. Move beyond the fear! Reach for the stars!

When you're sure the goal you're working towards is something you really want, is consistent with your values, and doesn't contradict any of your other goals, you have a much better chance of realising that goal, of getting the results you need and want.

CHAPTER 7

The Business of Happiness

Money doesn't make you happy. I now have $50 million but I was just as happy when I had $48 million.
—Arnold Schwarzenegger

Doing the work on your beliefs, strengths, and values and setting the right goals is serious business. You've done a lot of work on these, so congratulations! Happiness is also an equally important part of the mix. Life is more fulfilling and success more achievable when we come at things from a happier place.

It often takes a conscious effort to get to that place of happiness. It wasn't until I was in my twenties that I realised this. It happened the day after my birthday. I used to get sad on my birthday. I can't explain it. Even if I was happy the day before and the day after, I almost always felt sad on my actual birthday. One particular birthday really stands out. On the day I turned twenty-five, I went to work as usual. Nobody there knew it was my birthday, and I didn't tell them. After work, I drove home to my one-bed, brown apartment in a part of Dublin that was near work but where I knew nobody. I skipped dinner, closed my brown curtains (on a sunny mid-summers evening), turned on the TV, and watched the movie *Ghost*, which makes you cry even if you're happy. While I watched, I ate an entire box of chocolates (even the strawberry creams, which I hate) and cried my eyes out for hours and hours. It was a really, really sad evening for me. My family was in the west of Ireland, three hours away. My best friends were scattered across the world, and I was lonely. It's quite embarrassing even now, writing this story. It's not one that I have told many people. Until now.

Eventually, I fell asleep. When I awoke the next morning, I actually didn't feel sad (it wasn't my birthday anymore), just emotionally exhausted! But that miserable birthday was a turning point for me. I realised I had to make an effort to be happy in my adult life, including on my birthday. I wanted to be happy, to feel joy, the joy I used to feel naturally most of the time as a child and even through early adulthood. So I started to research happiness. I read books, had conversations, and attended seminars. I was going to crack the code for happiness!

So, Happiness—What's It All About?

I had all sorts of questions. Is happiness a luxury? (No) Do we deserve it? (Yes) Can happiness be learned? (Yes) How important is it anyway in life to be happy? (Very) Is it even *possible* to be truly happy? (Yes) What difference will a little more (or a lot more) happiness make? (A big difference) Are happier people more successful, more productive, more resilient, more creative? (Absolutely)

On a personal level, are you someone who is "happy" most of the time? Or are you someone who doesn't even identify with the word? (Many people believe that being on this earth is more about suffering than happiness.) Do you prefer to use a different word, like "contented," or maybe "satisfied," "normal," "doing okay"? Do you even think about happiness? One sure thing about the feeling of being happy, whether you use the actual word "happiness" or not, is that the concept and the feeling are different for each one of us. We all have our own formula for getting to that place of happiness. And remember—your happiness is *your* choice.

I placed this chapter on happiness in this location in the book because various studies have shown that when we approach our goals from a positive place, we set better goals and have a higher chance of achieving them too. So wherever you are on the happiness scale—whether you would like a little more or a lot more happiness (especially if you are feeling down—sad, lonely, low in energy)—where do you start? Where do you *actually* start? What do you actually have to do to live a happy life?

First, as with anything you do, you *decide* you're going to be happier on a daily basis and believe that you can be. With everything you do, taking the decision to actually do it is the first step in the process.

Do you remember having *fun* as a child? Do you remember experiencing laughter, giggles, and true joy regularly—often from simply running and playing in the fields or on your street with your friends? Why do we allow life to crush that joy from our being? Where does the "martyr syndrome" come from? Yes, we need to be responsible in life, we can't play all day, but does this mean that joy and happiness need to disappear from our lives? Unfortunately, for many, yes it does, but believe me—it's worth striving for. As with everything else, if you apply some of your energy to opening yourself up to joy and happiness, you can become happier and experience more joy. And, actually, finding joy and happiness doesn't need to cost very much, if anything at all.

Ah, the Joy of Happiness…

When you've decided that you're going to be happier, the first thing you need to do is get to really *know yourself—know what actually makes* you *happy.* You might think you know yourself already, but it's great to remind yourself every now and then of who you really are and what you actually want from life. It's easy to get sidetracked by others' values and expectations of you. So you need to constantly reassess what matters to *you*. What's important to *you*? Recently, one of my friend's four-year-old son left behind some "Match Attax" cards (cards from a popular football trading card game) in our house, and I popped them in the post to him. His mum was most appreciative, but, concerned at putting me to the trouble, she said it wasn't important, and I shouldn't have bothered sending the cards to her son. I told her I'd wanted to return the cards because they were important to *him*. He was absolutely delighted, especially, I think, about getting a letter in the post!

Can you remember times when you were at your happiest? Think about that time, or other times you've felt you're happiest. What brings *you* joy? This is a question I ask all my clients and have asked colleagues and friends over time. For most people, it's the simple things in life that don't cost anything—family time, being outdoors, finding that elusive hour on a Saturday afternoon for a quiet coffee. Ask yourself what brings you joy and answer honestly.

So often we look outwards to find peace, contentment, comfort, and passion, and we forget that we're actually more than able to provide these things for ourselves. We need to find our own happiness formula so the time spent on gaining self-knowledge and acquiring self-happiness will never be time wasted—and also so that those around us might feel happy in our presence. After all, happiness, like misery, can be infectious. I defy anyone to say that their families, especially their children, are truly happy when the mum is feeling sad and behaving accordingly. How do you think colleagues or employees at work feel when the boss is unhappy and unable to handle stress? Morale and results both suffer.

When you truly come to know yourself, you'll realise that nobody is perfect. That could be boring anyway! You'll come to accept that you're not. And because you know and value yourself, you'll begin striving to become the best person that *you* can be. As you come to know who you truly are, you will also gain a wonderful perspective about the world around you, and you will begin to see the world with a fresh set of eyes. With this comes the beautiful understanding of what is most important in life: love, family, and friends, and whatever is important to *you*. And living from that place of embracing who you are brings joy.

So, what is the key to genuine happiness? It varies from person to person, but there are some universal determinants of happiness. I have already mentioned exercise and getting enough sleep. Here are a few others:

1. **Smile.** Fake it until you make it! According to Charles Darwin, our emotional responses influence our feelings. Today, there's evidence that our facial expressions play a big role in our emotions. Research has proven that when a situation has you feeling stressed, unhappy, or flustered, even the most forced smile can decrease your stress levels and make you feel happier. Take this idea one step further to encompass laughter and love. What makes you laugh? Do more of it. Whom do you laugh with? Whom do you love? Spend more time with them.

2. **Practice gratitude**. Be thankful daily. A great idea for cultivating an "attitude of gratitude" is to start a gratitude journal and list three to five things each day that you're grateful for in your life. These could be any manner of things, from the compliment you received from your boss for a job well done to the unexpected bear hug given by a friend, the good night's sleep

you just had, your morning coffee—small things as well as the big stuff. Use this journal as a constant reminder of what you're really thankful for. Read it anytime you're feeling sad. This exercise works! Studies have shown that writing down three things you're grateful for, daily for twenty-one days, can retrain the brain to scan for the positive in the world, rather than the negative (Emmons and McCullough, 2003).

3. **Journal.** Writing down one positive experience every day allows your brain to relive it. You get to experience that feeling of gratitude all over again.

4. **Meditate.** Evidence shows that meditation can help improve our ability to focus and increase our alertness, academic performance, creativity, and happiness. Studies show that thirty minutes per day for eight weeks can reduce stress and increase memory and empathy. Twenty minutes per day for four days improves cognitive skills. Twenty minutes per day for three days results in a significant decrease in pain sensitivity. Even ten minutes a day for sixteen weeks significantly improves our ability to focus.

5. **Practice random (but conscious) acts of kindness.** Send an email to someone in your network to praise or thank them for something they've done. Pop a card in the post to a friend you haven't seen in a while. These acts of kindness will contribute to your own happiness. Doing something helpful for someone else can really take your mind away from dwelling on your own thoughts. It's just a great idea for so many reasons.

What's Your Happiness Formula?

I have decided that I actually want to be happy. I like happy feelings, but like most people, sometimes I feel sad. Often there's a reason, but sometimes there really isn't an external factor that I can pinpoint as the cause. Maybe hormones…But I'm not going to let hormones dictate my mood and waste my valuable time. Life is too short!

So I've developed a few of my own happiness formulas. I started with listing a few things I know about myself:

- I need seven to eight hours of sleep.
- Exercise, preferably outdoors, makes me happy.
- I'm sad when my daughter's sad (haven't quite managed to build that particular boundary!)
- I love meeting good friends.
- I need chocolate, not a huge amount. A little, regularly, does it for me.

Here are my formulas for sticking to what I need to be happy.

Formula #1 My Daily Guaranteed Happiness (H) Formula

H = Up by 6.30 + 2 × Water + Exercise (outdoors ± weather) + Family breakfast + Complete interesting tasks

Formula #2 Feeling a Little Sad Happiness Formula

H = Rise 7 a.m. + Run (outdoors) + Family breakfast + Meet friend + Do most interesting & helpful work + Healthy lunch + Dark chocolate[2]

The Formula

Formula #3 Feeling Very Sad Happiness Formula

> $H^{\cdot}$ = Get out of the house/office + Take a mountain hike or spa day with a good friend

Examples of other happiness formulas I've come across vary greatly; we're all different. For a certain person I know, the happiness formula below really works (it's very different from mine—back to the uniqueness):

> TH (True Happiness—on a regular day) = Thinking about cars, computers, business + Sleep late Saturday morning ∞ Drinks with the boys on Friday night

Another friend's formula looks like this:

> H = Time to self/hiking in the mountains with a good friend(s)/ reading & researching

Maybe yours could be like another formula I know:

> H = Family time + Three-day work week + Gourmet food + Yoga daily

I suggest creating your own happiness formulas. It's fun and can really help to increase your happiness levels.

Dig Deep to Find Your Joy

In denying ourselves happiness, we often deny happiness to those whom we love and cherish too. How many of you worry about a family member or a friend who is unhappy? If you can summon any resources at all within yourself that you can use to maximize your happiness, then I believe you must. If not, if you just can't do it, please ask someone you trust for help—you and those who love you deserve it. Anything you approach from a positive place—your home life, business, your health—is not only more enjoyable for you but also produces your best results.

The Earth will still spin, the Sun will still shine, and waves will crash on the beach long after you and I are gone. Make your time here matter. Enjoy the beauty and magnificence of our world. Be kind and generous of spirit. And be happy. As a pharmacist, I have often thought wouldn't it be great if there really was such a thing as a happy pill without a downside? Sadly, there isn't. Through life's challenges, continue to just practice being happy. It's a perfect world—effort in, result out. When you practice something regularly, you master it. Happiness is worth practicing.

As a starting point, ask yourself this question: what gives *me* joy? Take some time to answer it honestly; then act on it. Act *now*. To help you take action, turn the page to chapter 8.

CHAPTER 8

The DO IT Programme for Action and Results

Wherever you see a successful business, someone once made a courageous decision.
—Peter Drucker, educator and author

The DO IT process builds on the exercises you carried out in chapter 6. If you did that work and are now clear on the positive beliefs that serve you best—that is, if you've determined your strengths and values—and formulated your purpose statement and goals, you're in great shape. Now it's time to do something about it. Otherwise, all the exercises you've completed, all that work you've written down, will be like that book on the shelf you're always meaning to read but haven't yet had time to read. In fact, the DO IT process may indeed free up your time so you can get to read that book at last.

There are four steps to DO IT:

Decide—make decisions that matter.

Organise to get the results you need.

Implement your plans.

Treat yourself.

This process works for me, and it's proven highly effective with my clients. Plus, it works fast. You just decide to do it. So if you haven't already taken action on the goals you set in chapter 6, read on for some further help. And if you have set them, this chapter will help you streamline the process and ensure success.

Make Decisions That Matter

It's only when we make the decision to do something that it actually happens. Even then, we need to own the decision and take action. Whether the task is large or small, absolutely nothing gets done without a decision being made and an action being taken. For example, in the morning, the alarm goes off. You're not ready for that wake-up call, so you lie in bed thinking about getting up—or not. You may even fall back to sleep. Suddenly, in the blink of an eye, you move from indecision to the decision to get out of bed—then you do it. That spark suddenly appears. Action!

It's only when you decide to update your CV that you actually do it, when you decide to go to the gym today that it happens, and when you decide you've had enough of feeling a lack of confidence that you'll do something about it. The decision point is the turning point. But your decision needs to be right for you, or you'll never follow through.

I live near the sea, by a great kitesurfing area. Recently, I was taking an evening walk, enjoying the sunshine and watching all the kitesurfers with their brightly coloured kites. The vivid reds, greens, yellows, and purples looked so beautiful against the evening sky. I thought, *What a great feeling that must be…the speed, the freedom, being out on the water in the wind and sunshine after a day's work.* I imagined the energy-high these guys must have from all of it. *What a buzz!* As I passed people walking the other way, I heard snippets of conversations. A few times I overheard someone say what I'd been thinking: *Oh wow, that must be a great feeling.*

What stops us trying kitesurfing or whatever else would produce that great feeling? I wondered. Do we not want to enough? Then I realised why Step 1 of the DO IT process is so effective in helping us get the results we want. It's not just making the decision to go for it that helps us to achieve our goals; it's making a decision defined by our values and strengths. For example, while I really love the idea of kitesurfing, I'm not a strong-enough swimmer to stay safe in the ocean. So to get that amazing feeling I imagine kitesurfers have, I implement the DO IT process to decide what I actually want to do for that exercise high (usually a run, cycle, or long hike in the mountains), and then I DO IT.

Without knowing yourself, your beliefs and how they serve you, your values, and your purpose in life, it's easy to make the wrong decisions, that is, decisions that don't work out for you. When you put some time and energy into discovering this information about yourself, you're equipped with the knowledge to make really great decisions—the right ones for you.

For instance, if you're 100 percent clear that you value family time and being around while your children are growing up, you're not going to want to take a job that requires you to be away for weeks at a time, even if that job is a huge promotion. If you're not 100 percent clear about what's important to you, you may take a new role for the money and realise that decision wasn't right for you and that you would have preferred to work, and succeed, nearer to your home. It's worth taking a step back and reminding yourself what you value before making big decisions. Then you can gain the clarity you need to make the right ones.

There was a time when I was between careers, staying at home, looking after basic household tasks (which I hadn't done for many years). I started to feel bored, even a bit worthless. Finally, I reminded myself what was important to me. Spending time with my daughter and being able to look after my family in a positive manner were right up there, top of my list. I realised that my time off gave me a chance to do what was important to me and do it well. Taking care of my family started to feel worthwhile. Because I now placed a value on what I was doing, the negative feelings disappeared, and I felt happy that I was living life and being able to act according to what I personally valued. That time off work has passed now, and I'm so glad I was able to enjoy it while I had the chance.

Organise to Get the Results You Need

A useful way to get organised for any goal you set for yourself is to take a page and write that goal down. Then think about what the goal means to you—financially, emotionally, or in any other way. Does it align with your values? Ask yourself if the timing is right and be absolutely sure the goal is right for you.

Next, make a list of what's required for you to achieve that goal. Then remind yourself of how you perform at your best—remember the successes you listed in chapter 6 and your particular list of strengths that contributed to these successes. Highlight any items that don't align with your strengths; you'll want to assign those to someone else. Then highlight what's currently missing from your resources—it may be time, money, influence. When you're 100 percent committed to this particular goal, and you know it's the right thing to do, hire in the resources you need, and if you can't afford to do that, either upskill yourself or ask someone to help you out.

This is easy if you're an organised person; it maybe not so fun if you're not. I have a client who says he's really disorganised, yet he's a successful retailer. He gets things done—how is this? He's lucky enough to employ the services of an extremely patient and organised PA. But what if you don't have the luxury of being able to do this? When your actions are leading you towards a meaningful goal, organising can become easier—try it! When the decision is right for you, you'll be so motivated that you'll be able to find the solutions to make it happen. And, it's okay to go through a revolving set of methods for being organised—phone-diary, notebook and highlighter marker, Post-it lists—whatever works for you at the time is great.

Implement Your Plans

If the list doesn't become actions, then nothing changes. A prioritised list that you're comfortable with is a must.

How will you do it?

- Decide that you will take a certain action; that's always the first step. You've already taken this step by now.
- Timetable it. Working to deadlines really helps move things forward so you get the results you're looking for.
- Write down the tasks so you can enjoy the pleasure of crossing them off your list when it's done.
- Tell someone out loud that you're going for this goal—someone who will help and encourage you. Another potential benefit of telling someone is that many of us feel honour bound to deliver when we've committed to someone else.
- Start with the tasks that can benefit you the most. Often, small changes can produce big results. Think of a plane going

off course by one or two degrees, yet ending up many kilometres from its intended destination. Or a sales team. If every salesperson on a team of six people makes just one extra sales call per day, that's thirty extra customers visited per week—guaranteed higher sales.

- What happens if you don't implement? Nothing changes. What happens if you do? You'll be a lot closer to getting the results you need.

Treat Yourself

Okay, so now you're working smart, you're focused on your goals, and you're achieving them. How will you reward yourself? Funny how rewards, when we've earned them, are even sweeter than when we don't. To quote William Shakespeare, "If all the year were playing holidays; To sport would be as tedious as to work." But, oh boy, when you've spent a long week at your desk, at meetings, run that marathon, climbed that mountain, or even spent a full weekend minding kids, and you're all stuck inside because of heavy rainfall, as often happens in Ireland, that reward is welcome.

People often joke with me that the health, wellness, and beauty industry must benefit hugely from my coaching clients who reward themselves for achieving their goals. It's probably true. In fact, it's definitely true—along with travel companies. When I ask my clients what they would choose as a reward for a job well done—what brings them joy—many say exercising—taking a walk, going to a yoga class, or blocking out time on a Saturday morning for a long cycle. Others book a massage, treat themselves to a facial, or indulge in a manicure. And then there are those who, after a particular goal has been reached, will book that holiday, or perhaps even buy that new car.

Remember, it's as important to put the "treat" on your To Do list as it is to write everything else there.

The benefits of treating yourself are more than just giving yourself a reward. When you look after yourself, you're better positioned to be kind and generous to others. Plus, rewarding yourself, depending on your choice of a reward, often offers time to reflect. We need times of reflection to perform at our best. It's when we're happy and relaxed that most of our best ideas about life and work come to us, ideas that can help us become unstuck and find solutions to seemingly unanswerable problems—as though the clutter has been cleared from our brain. Some of these ideas can spark new intentions. And then, achieving the next goal is just around the corner!

CHAPTER 9

Habits, Habits, Habits, Habits, Habits

Successful people are simply those with successful habits.
—Brian Tracy, author and leadership trainer

When you practice anything—whether it's running, delivering keynotes, preparing spreadsheets, cultivating healthy habits, or working towards happiness—you'll become better at it. Your increased skill will build your confidence in whatever it is you're trying to master. For example, if you decide to practice happiness, you'll become happier, which can help you become more successful. According to Shawn Achor, author of *The Happiness Advantage*, "When we are positive, our brains become more engaged, creative, motivated, energetic, resilient, and productive at work."

When you feel happier, you feel like spreading the happiness, being kinder to others. And then others will be more kind and helpful to you, which in turn increases your happiness…it's a self-perpetuating circle.

Healthy Habits

Just as knowing yourself, connecting to your beliefs, strengths, and values, is the foundation for better decisions, self-awareness is also essential to choosing better habits. At the same time, there are some habits worth adopting even while you're working on your beliefs, strengths, values, and sense of purpose, because they'll support your work.

Exercise is one of these habits. Eating healthy is another, as is getting enough sleep.

Exercise

So many people say they want to exercise more, need to exercise more, yet they don't. Perhaps it's the effort involved in actually getting out for that run, into the gym, or on that bicycle that stops them. In my case, even though I love cycling, I sometimes find the effort of getting ready—strapping on my helmet, pulling on my cycling shoes, finding my cycling glasses, filling my water bottle, retrieving my bike from under someone else's—enough to make me change my mind and stay at home (even though it doesn't seem like a lot to do when I read it written down here!). However, with running or walking, there are fewer obstacles. I just need to put on my running shoes and leave the house—it's that much easier. So I run more than I cycle.

I have a friend who finds it really difficult to get herself out of the house to exercise, yet she enjoys the feeling afterwards so much that she has asked her husband to order her out for a run before breakfast three times a week. It works for her, and her whole family benefits from her good mood. So finding the type of exercise (and maybe the right "coach," as my friend did) is key to embedding a new habit and incorporating it into your routine.

And in the case of exercise, you want to find what works, because here's the thing—while "exercise" may be a dirty word for you, it has so many indisputable advantages that it's critical to include it in your life. Here are a few of the many benefits:

- When you go for a walk or visit the gym, you're out of the house, away from the temptation of snacks.
- You release endorphins, which are happiness-inducing hormones.
- You feel good about yourself, a sense of achievement.
- This good feeling often results in healthier eating patterns.
- You'll increase clarity and aha moments, which come during times of reflection and often during exercise, not when your head is down at work.

There's a lot about exercise in this chapter, and you may ask why. Well, in addition to the benefits I've already listed, exercise increases optimism, boosts heart and brain health, increases energy, speeds up metabolism, and soothes stress—all of which help you perform at your best and get the results you want. And as I mentioned in the first bullet point, when you're exercising, you're away from the kitchen. (Yep, the kitchen is not the best place to exercise.)

Exercise is great if you love it, but what if you don't? One useful trick is to start with whatever form of exercise seems the easiest for you. A ten-minute walk for example. Or how about taking the stairs every time there's an option to choose between stairs and the lift? Can you get off the bus one or two stops farther away from your place of work? Would you prefer to exercise while watching TV? Is hiring a personal trainer the best and only way to get you started?

A recent study I carried out on joy and where people find joy in their lives showed that overwhelmingly joyous feelings come when people are with family or good friends, exercising outdoors, appreciating nature and a beautiful view, listening to birds singing—the simple pleasures in life. Where do you find your joy? A good first step is to incorporate exercise into finding your joy? Walk to the place with the beautiful view, jog with a friend, or play in the garden or park with your children. Most parents, including me at times, don't often feel like kicking a ball around a park. Yet every single time I agree to kicking a ball around a park, I have a really wonderful, joyous time. It ticks so many boxes—family time, exercise, being outdoors. And we often reward ourselves with an ice cream or popcorn afterwards—what's not to like about that?

So it helps to know where you find joy; then if you really don't love to exercise, you can just incorporate it into your joyous moments. I have a client who doesn't like exercise. He finds joy in "thinking about airplanes." He was the one exception in my Joy survey, since thinking is his favourite activity. He used to enjoy cycling, so he now cycles to his local airport, with his binoculars and spots planes, 11 km each way—the perfect solution—three in one: exercise, thinking about airplanes, and looking at airplanes. Maybe you find joy in shopping. If so, why not walk to the stores or get off the public transport a few stops early? Or you could even park your car farther away from the stores and walk. And if you like fashion, wear flat, old shoes so you'll have a great reason to buy a great new pair plus a large new handbag in which to put your new shoes. Also, because you'll have a clear head after walking, you won't be as likely to make purchasing decisions you may later regret, which will save money. Ah, the multitude of benefits of exercise…

If you decide exercise is important enough (and it really, really is), there are many ways you can incorporate it into an already busy life. Decide to do so, and find a way to make it fun.

Eating Well

Eating well is also important. We are what we eat; therefore we need to eat to suit our body, which requires a degree of self-awareness about how your body reacts to certain foods. Once again, you need to know yourself. Sometimes food intolerances can contribute to stress in your body and interfere with sleep, energy, and well-being. If you have weight issues, low energy levels, bloating, skin problems—all of which interfere with high performance—it's a great idea to carry out a proper food intolerance test to find out if something you regularly consume is having an adverse effect on your body. If there are two or three food items your system can't tolerate, it's relatively easy these days to find suitable substitutes.

If you need to lose or manage weight, read the food labels. Decide to always buy the options that contain less sugar and fat; many of them taste the same or even better. You can still eat the meals you like, with little or no sacrifice at all. If your career means that you eat mainly at work, identify the times of day that pose the highest temptation and bring a healthy, tasty snack with you to have for those times.

And don't forget to drink plenty of water. Hydration is a habit people say they struggle with. We all know we should drink more water, yet so many times, 8:00 p.m. comes and we haven't drunk nearly as much as we need to. Here's an idea: bring two large glasses of water to bed, ready to drink the minute you wake up every morning. It's surprisingly easy to get into this habit, and you're a quarter of the way there with hydration before the day really begins.

Sleep

We also need a proper night's sleep (seven to eight hours) most nights to perform at our best. Dr. Allan Rechtschaffen performed an experiment with lab rats to demonstrate the lethal consequences of long-term sleep deprivation. During the experiment, sleep-deprived rats developed sores, lost weight despite eating more than usual, and suffered a drop in body temperature. After thirty-two days, all the rats were dead. The upshot of the experiment is that as we deprive ourselves of sleep—an hour here, a half hour there—we expose ourselves to the same risks as the rats.

On a lighter note, Arianna Huffington's 2010 talk at TEDWomen, "How to Succeed? Get More Sleep" is definitely worth watching. In her speech, she urges women to say no to the cult of sleep deprivation and lead a new revolution based on getting enough sleep. "Women," she says, "we are literally going to sleep our way to the top. Literally."

If sleep is an issue for you, cut out caffeine in the afternoon, get that exercise habit going, and perhaps meditate or listen to a relaxing meditation or yoga *nidra* (yogic sleep) shortly before bedtime.

You can also try the Yes/No technique. I find this useful when tempted to have a late-afternoon caffeine fix. If I say "yes" to that cuppa, I'm definitely saying "no" to a good night's sleep. This technique really focuses the mind. It's simply to ask yourself, "If I say yes to this, what am I saying no to?" And vice versa. It's a great tool if you are someone who finds it hard to say no. One of my clients is a CEO of a large global organisation and a board member of various other companies. He's extremely busy and tries to please people all the time, so he finds the Yes/No technique particularly useful. He has a very full diary, so now when someone asks him for a meeting at a certain time, he'll pause and ask himself the Yes/No scenario. If he says Yes to this meeting, at this particular time, what is he saying No to? This question is really great for making decisions about what's best for you: TV versus yoga, pastry versus feeling good in your clothes, preparing for that meeting versus relaxing now but worrying about it too.

Speed Up Good Habit Formation

A friend of mine, who is an excellent chiropractor, once gave me an excellent tip for speeding up good habit formation. I needed to improve my posture because my shoulders were constantly sore from sitting too long hunched up at my desk. He said, "Just straighten up and pull your shoulders back every time you walk through a door." At first, I remembered only sometimes, but I quickly remembered more often, and straightening up and pulling my shoulders back became a habit. Now it's easy.

Once you've prioritized the habits you want to form and have selected the easiest ones to start with, you can set a daily reminder on your phone for whenever you've decided you are going to take the appropriate action.

Practical Tools to Embed Habits

In *The Power of Habit*, author Charles Duhigg tells us that neuroscientists have identified that our habit-making behaviours happen in a part of the brain called the basal ganglia, which also plays a key role in the development of emotions, memories, and pattern recognition. Decisions, though, are made in a different part of the brain called the prefrontal cortex. As soon as a behaviour becomes automatic, the decision-making part of your brain goes into a sleep mode of sorts. I completely get this—and it became especially obvious to me when writing this book. Almost every hour, without even thinking, I had developed a habit of snacking. My prefrontal cortex was definitely asleep, being overruled by the basal ganglia.

"In fact, the brain starts working less and less," says Charles Duhigg. "The brain can almost completely shut down…And this is a real advantage, because it means you have all of this mental activity you can devote to something else."

So what do you want to be better at? Is it being a better CEO, public speaking, negotiating, preparing accurate cash flows (a matter very close to my heart after so many years in business), or running long distance? Have you identified what's stopping you? Is it fear of the unknown or fear of failure, lack of experience, laziness, or worry about what others may think?

Doing the exercises outlined in chapter 6 can really help you connect with exactly what you want. You then have the canvas on which your decisions are painted. Next, you can use the DO IT formula from chapter 8 to implement those actions. Then get ready for these positive changes. Along the way, be kind to yourself, eat well, get enough rest, and spend time with the people with whom you share joy.

The Daily Five Thank Yous

One particular tool I have used for many years that friends, colleagues, clients, and I find useful to provide that almost-instant spark to take your mind from a less positive to a positive, "can-do" place, essential for the formation of good habits, is a very simple daily routine that I call the "Daily Five Thank Yous."

You can say the Five Thank Yous throughout the day. When you wake up each morning, before you even get out of bed, say, "thank you" for the things in your life that you appreciate. I keep this list simple: Thank you for a good night's sleep, the comfy bed, the fact that that I organised my work clothes last night…It doesn't have to be complicated or deep. The action of switching your mind to an attitude of gratitude means that your day has instantly started on a more positive note.

In the car on the way to work (I've practiced this for years, and, oh boy, it's useful!), I say thank you for at least five things. Again, I keep it simple. I say thank you for the good night's sleep, the lovely cup of tea (the first cup is always the best), the nice day, the hug from my daughter, the green traffic lights. I may thank myself for actually remembering to pack my lunch, as I often forget! If I ran early that morning, I say thanks for that. If I didn't run, I say thanks for the extra half hour in bed.

Always be 100 percent truthful with yourself and only say thank you for things that you are actually grateful for. For the morning Thank Yous, I find it helpful to be specific and not get into generalities that we can all recite when sometimes put on the spot; we may be thankful for our families, but I find it more helpful to be specific. For instance, I sometimes say, "thank you" for not being awakened during the night by a snoring husband!

I recommend saying the Five Thank Yous any time you feel stressed or under pressure. During a particularly stressful work day, it's good to find a space away from your desk, take a few deep breaths, and remind yourself of the good things that happened that day. There will always be a few.

The Five Thanks Yous are also great for unwinding. Often at night, when you're tired, when the stress and unhappy feelings can hit, saying the Five Thank Yous can make you feel better. After a really busy day, when you're tired and weary, your mind won't calm down, and it's difficult to sleep, they can calm your brain. Or before you go to bed, writing down and then repeating the Five Thank Yous can help you get to sleep quicker.

Once more, I find that being thankful for things that happened *that day* is the best. After a few days of this exercise, no matter how stressful your life is, you realise there's something in every day to be grateful for—things like a nice phone call from a friend, a tasty dinner, a lovely hot shower, a laugh with a colleague. Even in stressful times, it's possible to find moments to be thankful for.

Friends, clients, and colleagues tell me they use this tool when they feel particularly fed up with life, and that within a very short time, not only does expressing gratitude become a habit, but they start appreciating life again, which makes the hard times easier. Try it and see. This practice takes absolutely no time out of your day.

Choose Habits That Matter

Another straightforward, yet essential habit-building tip that can really make the difference when incorporating habits into your life is to revisit your beliefs, strengths, and values when you're prioritising the habits you want to incorporate. Choose the habits that matter most to you; these are the easiest ones to build into your daily routine. As your well-being improves, and your new habits deliver the energy and focus necessary to reach your larger goals, the probability of achieving the results you want increases. After prioritising habits, start with whatever's easiest for you. Get rid of the obstacles that are keeping you from building better habits

Build Routines

The secret to creating good habits is to build your routines so that when you really need them, they'll be there for you—like, no matter when you have to do a big presentation, you block out time in your diary to prepare—just in case you need it, for those last-minute changes. According to a 2009 study conducted in the UK by Phillippa Lally and colleagues, it takes, on average, sixty-six days to embed a new habit. Initially, that may seem a long time; however, sixty-six days, just a little more than two months, can and does pass quickly. However, for simple habits, such as the Five Thank Yous, drinking more water, and getting to work a half hour earlier, simply *deciding* to take action and *doing* these tasks can happen immediately. Decide to build these new actions into your routine.

For example, to build the habit of drinking more water, make placing two glasses of water on your nightstand before going to bed (so you'll drink it in the morning) part of your nightly routine. To build the habit of saying The Five Thank Yous, stick a note to your car dashboard, so you can say them to yourself en route to work every morning. Whatever you decide you want to make into a habit, take the necessary steps to build it into your daily routine. Very quickly, it can become second nature to you—a habit.

There are two more easy habits that you can build into your routine that can help you feel really great. One is to perform a little (or large if you like) act of kindness for someone every day. It doesn't have to take much time or cost anything. It's amazing how being kind to others can lessen your focus on yourself and whatever's holding you back. It feels great, so why not try it? Praise someone for a job well done. Make that stressed colleague a cup of coffee. Call that friend whom you know would love to hear from you. Send a surprise card to someone you're thankful for. It's a good idea to set a reminder on your phone for a certain time every day until the actions become second nature.

The other habit is meditation. This doesn't have to be a serious, formal action—standing away from your desk, looking out the window (if you have one), and clearing your mind of thoughts for a few minutes can help. Of course, setting aside five or ten minutes to meditate when you're relaxed and calm is even better. When you sit down to meditate, to get started, think of something nice. I say this to my daughter sometimes when she finds it hard to get to sleep. The same thing works for meditation—it actually doesn't have to be any more complicated than that. Notice as thoughts come and go. And they will. Try not to latch on to the thoughts; just let them float by. Be gentle with yourself as you explore a meditative practice. As you learn to let your thoughts go, your brain will become calmer, and you'll find that your mind eventually clears and you are indeed meditating.

I suggest taking things a week at a time and measuring your progress every day and again every week. I'm not telling you anything you don't already know somewhere deep inside. Our habits and behaviours are how we express ourselves in the world and deeply influence who we are and how we feel about ourselves—and others. When you're happier, you and those around you are happier. When you perform better at work, you and so many others benefit too.

So how do you ensure that you build these useful habits? It comes back to you *deciding* to make the changes you need. Expressing gratitude, showing kindness, and meditating can put you in touch with who you are and increase your ability to make good decisions. When the decisions you make feel right to you, you're more likely to build the habits—because these choices matter to you. When you start getting the results you want, you'll uncover the evidence that the changes you have made actually work; you'll find the confidence you need to keep going. These changes can help you get the results you need and want.

Daily, Weekly, Monthly Action Plan for Embedding Better Habits

No matter what your goals are—and everyone's goals are different—measuring your progress will really speed up good habit formation. Below is the simple plan I use and find effective. These actions, listed below, just take a few minutes every day. You can formulate your own plan that works for you.

Your Daily Action Plan

1.	Twenty minutes of exercise (absolute minimum).
2.	The three things I did today that made me feel good/furthered the business/family, that is, honoured my values.
3.	Five- to ten-minute meditation.
4.	The Five Thank Yous.
5.	One small (or large!) act of generosity.

Your Weekly Action Plan

1.	Set/review goals and progress.
2.	Do one enjoyable thing for yourself every week. Believe that you deserve it. You do.

Your Monthly Action Plan

1.	Review your progress.
2.	Plan for the next thirty days.

3.	Take some extra time to relax (in whatever way suits you best).
4.	Celebrate your successes.

Just as knowing yourself and what matters to you is essential for setting achievable goals, knowing the make-up of your habits is key to changing them for the better. What are the triggers? What are the underlying causes? And, crucially, what rewards would help you stay on track?

We know what needs to be done, and we want to make changes, yet it's not so easy. It's definitely best to start with habits that matter to you, because they'll be the easiest. Even changing one small habit for a better one can pay dividends. You have the option of setting reminders or asking a friend or trusted colleague for help. And remember—it's okay to slip up every now and then; practically everyone does. It's not a reason to give up though. Tomorrow is a new day, and, as Eleanor Roosevelt said, "With the new day comes new strength and new thoughts."

Remember—all actions become habits when we practice them. So why not take it, as the old Country and Western song goes, "one day at a time."

CHAPTER 10

Result: Connected to Your Success

Success is not final; failure is not fatal: It is the courage to continue that counts.
—Winston S. Churchill

Congratulate yourself for your success in getting as far as you have, in life, business, sport—wherever you are! At this point, it's a good time to think about what success means for you, because success means something different for everyone. And sometimes once you achieve that success, you realise it doesn't look the way you pictured it would. It doesn't feel right. This can happen if your goal in the first place didn't come from a place of being truly connected to what you wanted and clear that it was right for you. You may have gotten the result in one area of your life but it came at too high a cost to another. For instance, career success can sometimes come at a cost to health or family and vice versa. But does it have to be like this? I believe it does not. Doing the exercises in this book can help you find out whether the result you're looking for is the right one for you, the one you actually want, that will mean something to you. The process of reaching that outcome is so much more fulfilling if you enjoy it along the way—if it matters to you.

Before I learned about these exercises, I always believed I was an accidental entrepreneur. It used to stress me that I'd chosen the "wrong path" because I constantly imagined my "better life" as a corporate leader, swanning around from one important meeting to another, travelling the world all the time. Or sometimes, when I was overwhelmed with life's responsibilities, I imagined myself as a bohemian traveller, roving from place to place with my (fashionable, cool) backpack (always in the sunshine and often with a surfboard on a beach in Hawaii). I was missing out! In reality—and I discovered this when I did the work on my beliefs, strengths, and values and formulated my purpose statement—I wouldn't be suited to either of those lives at all—for so many reasons. I really value independence, like to choose my own schedule when at all possible, and love a challenge. Surfing in Hawaii would provide a challenge for a while, but when I had mastered that (and while I have learned to surf, I haven't surfed in Hawaii—*yet*), I'd just be looking for the next challenge, probably a mental one. Also, I prefer to design my own travel schedule around family commitments. So, entrepreneurship has turned out to be perfect for me. What's perfect for you?

Get Out Your Spade and Dig Deep

It can be difficult to dig deep inside yourself and answer absolutely honestly the questions you've been asked in this book. But it's important. Often our choices can be consciously or subconsciously influenced by others—friends, family, neighbours, colleagues, by society in general. But when you connect with yourself, when you truly know what you desire and what aligns with your desires, it's like a weight being lifted from your shoulders. Really, believe me, when you've done the work on knowing *your* values and have taken the decision to honour your values with your daily actions, life can be fab.

When I was running my wholesale-distribution business, I worked with big global beauty brands, including St Tropez, Smashbox, OPI, and Neal's Yard Remedies, which was all really exciting. (I got to swan around a bit to "important" meetings in fabulous places!) I learned so much, met lots of very interesting people, and overcame challenges regularly. I loved so many aspects of that business; however, running that business did not fully allow me to live life in accordance with my values.

I remember one Friday afternoon after we'd spent most of the week trying to get a shipment of shampoo delivered for a retailer promotion—a big customer, with stores throughout the country. Despite huge effort on our part and the part of our freight-forwarding company, the shipment hadn't arrived due to circumstances completely out of our control—a hurricane. The entire time I was in the distribution business, most deliveries arrived in plenty of time for us to get the stock to the retailer's shelves according to agreed timelines, but every year, one or two shipments were delayed for various reasons. We learned to allow more time for shipping at certain times of year, but every now and then, fate intervened—the order wouldn't be ready or the products we really needed were short-shipped. All part of the day to day. All usually manageable.

But that Friday, when the ship carrying the shampoo didn't dock on time, the buyer for the chain of stores was really angry and threatened to take every single item from our company off their shelves, shouted, screamed, and called our company all sorts of unmentionable names. We'd done everything possible to try to get the shipment in on time, reroute it, and fly it in a separate order. We'd even offered the retailer all sorts of compromises. Nothing worked in this particular case. It didn't do *our* business any good either when a hurricane delayed our deliveries to customers! Even after we explained all that happened—the hurricane—this was still a "disaster."

Once we'd had the conversation with the buyer and recovered from the verbal abuse, I remember sitting at my desk and thinking, *Wow, what on earth am I doing with my life when a late shipment of shampoo is a "disaster"?* Of course, I understood the buyer was under huge pressure, and yes, we had an agreement, which we really tried hard to honour, but even so, the reaction was out of the ordinary.

I also remember thinking on that afternoon that even though I didn't want to be going through what I was actually going through at that moment, the buyer's job must have been even more stressful for a lack of shampoo to have elicited such a reaction. That was one of *many* moments in life that gave me food for thought and brought me back to remembering what's important, which, to me, is family, health, a job well done (a challenge overcome), friends, fun, and finding joy. I didn't make any major changes on that particular day, just filed the learning away in my brain for future use—sometimes, it takes a number of experiences that are contrary to our values to spark the decision to act.

Where's Your Joy?

When I conducted the survey on "What brings you joy?" some people were actually surprised about what brought them joy in life. Many people hadn't even thought about it before. I asked this question to people whose ages ranged from eleven to eighty-seven—men and women, entrepreneurs, corporate leaders, teachers, people who are healthy and people who are not so well, clients, and friends. As I mentioned in chapter 9, overwhelmingly, it was the simple things in life that brought people joy. So when setting goals and looking for results, remember that to be successful, you need to connect within to who you really are and be sure that what you target as your goal is indeed yours—what brings you joy—and nobody else's.

Be Delighted with Who You Are

No matter who you are, life won't be perfect. Nobody's life is absolutely perfect. Being connected to who you are and clear about what you want in life can help you live a life of resilience, where failure is a learning experience, not the end of the world, where what you do matters to you—a life filled with happiness and success.

It's great to be able to bounce back when things don't go your way. Being happy with who you are usually means you are not so hard on yourself when things go wrong and you are more open to options and opinions. Earlier in this book, I mentioned a salesperson who really valued customer relationships. She was so clear on who she was and what was important to her. She also valued clarity. When she looked at her annual, monthly, weekly, and daily sales targets, she instantly worked out which customers she needed to sell to and how much, to reach her sales goal. However, if something unexpected happened, she never let it get her down. She went immediately to Plan B and even Plan C when necessary. She came to me with ideas and suggestions—and was also a team player; she helped others too. She was connected to her success because she lived and worked in accordance with her values, and the whole company benefitted as a result.

Each moment in life is precious, never to be repeated. Every person we meet has his or her own story, each of equal value. Everyone has their ups and downs, and often we have no idea what's going on for other people. We can misjudge situations, take offence when someone doesn't say hi and smile, or take a casual comment personally. More often than not, the behaviour of others has nothing to do with us. So why do we make our choices based on what others think?

I know for sure that not one of my friends is my friend because of where I live, my chosen career path, how I raise my daughter, or what car I drive. We're friends because we connect with one another; we support and listen to one another; and, crucially, we share fun, adventures, and laughter together. There's a lovely freedom in knowing that. For each one of you who has read this book, I wish you the freedom to make your own choices, from a place of real, authentic connection to your inner self, and to, therefore, get the results that serve *you* best in life.

Live Life with Greater Ease

When I worked as a business and executive coach, people often told me they would simply like to live their lives with greater ease. As I mentioned earlier, sometimes business success can come at too high a price where family, health, and personal well-being are concerned, yet many people want to work and make a success of their career or business and still have time and energy for other areas of their lives. It's possible to make changes that create more ease in your life. To do so, you can start with the smallest, easiest changes you can make—changes where you start to feel the benefits almost immediately. When you feel the benefits, you'll be encouraged to continue to make more ambitious changes, leading you towards embedding better habits and living your life with greater ease.

I hope you'll find this book helpful in doing just that. I hope you'll also keep this book close to hand, so you can return to it whenever you feel stuck or need help with another change you'd like to make.

Just remember—clarity is key. When you're clear on your own purpose, confidence and conviction can then follow. You'll get the results you want; when you want them; and more important, they'll be the right results for you, your family, your business, and your life.

I wish you well in your endeavours. It's truly possible to live the life you dream of—to scale your business, to travel the world, to be your very best in whatever you choose to do.

Acknowledgements

I am grateful to my husband, Niall, for believing I could write this book and for his meticulous review. He mentioned that I should write a book some years ago and didn't give up encouraging me until the final word was written. I would also like to thank my daughter, Holly, for her patience while I sat at my computer, day after day, and especially for her suggestions for the book cover.

Thank you so much to my editor, Kelly Malone, who, when she read my first draft, also told me she believed I could do it. As Kelly is based in Seattle and I'm in Ireland, we had a wonderful twenty-four-hour operation going for a few months. Most importantly, we had fun with it. Thank you, too, to Lisa Tener, author and book-writing coach, for recommending Kelly as my editor.

I also want to thank all the participants in my Confidence and Joy surveys. I appreciate your time and openness. And thank you to fellow coach, Emer Daly, for working on the Confidence survey with me.

A final thank you to all the people who listened to me and have helped me make this book possible.

Please Review

Dear Reader,

If you enjoyed this book, would you kindly post a short review on whichever platform you purchased from? Your feedback will make all the difference to getting the word out about this book.

Thank you in advance.

www.ingramcontent.com/pod-product-compliance
Lightning Source LLC
Chambersburg PA
CBHW071420070526
44578CB00003B/639